An Ireland Worth Working For

An Ireland Worth Working For

Towards a New Democratic Programme

Tom Healy

NEW ISLAND

AN IRELAND WORTH WORKING FOR
First published in 2019 by
New Island Books
16 Priory Hall Office Park
Stillorgan
County Dublin
Republic of Ireland
www.newisland.ie

Print ISBN: 978-1-84840-724-4
Ebook ISBN: 978-1-84840-725-1

A CIP catalogue record for this book is available from the British Library.

Typeset (text and graphs) by JVR Creative India
Cover design by Kate Gaughran
Trade union printed by Johnswood Press Ltd, Tallaght, Dubin 24

www.NERInstitute.net

New Island Books is a member of Publishing Ireland.

Dedicated to all who are working and caring
for the future of the island of Ireland.

Without a vision the people perish.
– Proverbs 29:18

You see things; and you say 'Why?'
But I dream things that never were;
and I say 'Why not?'
– George Bernard Shaw

At the time of publication, the matter of Brexit and the details of the United Kingdom's transition to a new relationship with the European Union was unresolved. Nevertheless, throughout this book, the author has assumed that the United Kingdom will leave the European Union one way or another.

Acknowledgements

While I write this book in my capacity as director of the Nevin Economic Research Institute (NERI), it does not necessarily reflect the views of the NERI or those of trade unions in general. I wish to acknowledge the support, advice and feedback of the NERI and other colleagues, including the following: John Barry, David Begg, Patricia King, Tom McDonnell, Louisa O'Brien and Michael Taft. In particular, I acknowledge the financial contribution towards this publication by a number of trade unions. I am also grateful for the help of colleagues of the institute for a stream of published articles and working papers that provided most of the empirical evidence required in preparing this book. Finally, I would like to thank the team at New Island Books and Djinn von Noorden for their diligent professional help in the editing and preparation of this book.

Contents

Foreword

The inaugural meeting of the First Dáil Éireann took place on 21 January 1919 in a world recovering from World War I, a collision of empires that caused the deaths of millions and injured countless more. It was a war that was slow to end and it was followed by the Great Flu, which swept away further millions in Europe. Yet for all the suffering and sadness that had been endured it was a moment of hope, a moment in which peoples across the world were imagining a new future, one founded on the right to national self-determination and upon economic and social justice.

From Belfast to Berlin, the trade union movement was on the march, winning new rights and confronting ancient injustices, advancing the rights of workers and expanding the horizons of the possible. From India to Egypt, peoples sought national independence, not for its own sake, but to define a new, more expansive vision of freedom.

The Democratic Programme of the First Dáil formed part of, and was a response to, those great movements of thought and action. It remains a foundational document in our democracy, one inspired by the spirit of James Connolly and the rhetoric of Patrick Pearse. Yet, despite the pragmatic and systemic nature of the Democratic Programme, it remains, in many respects, a promise yet to be fulfilled.

The last decade has been a difficult one for the island of Ireland. We have witnessed the failure of one model of economic and social development, in Ireland and in the European Union, but have yet to resolve or decide, collectively, upon a new, alternative path towards economic and social progress. The challenges we face today are immense and they are as pressing as those that confronted our forebears a century ago. Our resilience is called for now, as well as a sophisticated evaluation of our founding models and assumptions. We need to acknowledge the limits of models that cannot bridge the appropriate relationship between the market and social security, cohesion, sustainability, justice and rights not fulfilled.

Our society is still marked by grave inequalities of income, wealth, opportunity and power, which prevent many of our citizens from realising their full potential. Our economy still reinforces some of those inequalities instead of mitigating them. Our people and our planet are threatened by the biodiversity loss, environmental degradation and, above all, by the potentially catastrophic consequences of climate change.

Now, more than ever, we need a renewed study of economics and political economy, one capable, in a gendered, socially fulfilling way, of analysing and understanding these challenges and of mobilising informed public action to address them.

This volume is an important contribution to the debate in which we must now engage on our shared island. It provides an analysis of how and why our economic model failed and constructs a framework for understanding how our economy functions – and should function – as well as an incisive perspective on the future of our relationship with the European Union and the changing relationship between labour and capital.

Most importantly, Tom Healy offers a series of proposals to realise the Democratic Programme in the twenty-first century. These proposals are comprehensive in scope, covering industrial policy, social protection, taxation, healthcare and education. I hope they will be debated and discussed both within the trade union movement and wider Irish society and, above all, that they will inspire action on policy and trigger the sort of engaged participation we need.

We must seek, as a great philosopher once said, not only to understand the world but to change it. We must strive to do so with creativity, informed intellect, generous sharing and warm hearts. May there be many more publications like this valuable contribution and the widest debates.

Michael D. Higgins
President of Ireland

The Democratic Programme

January 1919[1]

We declare in the words of the Irish Republican Proclamation the right of the people of Ireland to the ownership of Ireland, and to the unfettered control of Irish destinies to be indefeasible, and in the language of our first President, Pádraig Mac Phiarais, we declare that the Nation's sovereignty extends not only to all men and women of the Nation, but to all its material possessions, the Nation's soil and all its resources, all the wealth and all the wealth-producing processes within the Nation, and with him we reaffirm that all right to private property must be subordinated to the public right and welfare.

We declare that we desire our country to be ruled in accordance with the principles of Liberty, Equality, and Justice for all, which alone can secure permanence of Government in the willing adhesion of the people.

We affirm the duty of every man and woman to give allegiance and service to the Commonwealth, and declare it is the duty of the Nation to assure that every citizen shall have opportunity to spend his or her strength and faculties in the service of the people. In return for willing service, we, in the name of the Republic of Ireland, declare the right of every citizen to an adequate share of the produce of the Nation's labour.

It shall be the first duty of the Government of the Republic of Ireland to make provision for the physical, mental and spiritual well-being of the children, to secure that no child shall suffer hunger or cold from lack of food, clothing, or shelter, but that all shall be provided with the means and facilities requisite for their proper education and training as Citizens of a Free and Gaelic Ireland.

The Irish Republic fully realises the necessity of abolishing the present odious, degrading and foreign Poor Law System, substituting therefor a sympathetic native scheme for the care of the Nation's aged and infirm, who shall not be regarded as a burden, but rather entitled to the Nation's gratitude and consideration. Likewise it shall be the duty of the Republic of Ireland to take such measures as will safeguard the health of the people and ensure the physical as well as the moral well-being of the Nation.

It shall be our duty to promote the development of the Nation's resources, to increase the productivity of its soil, to exploit its mineral deposits, peat bogs, and fisheries, its waterways and harbours, in the interests and for the benefit of the Irish people.

It shall be the duty of the Republic of Ireland to adopt all measures necessary for the recreation and invigoration of our Industries, and to ensure their being developed on the most beneficial and progressive co-operative and industrial lines. With the adoption of an extensive Irish Consular Service, trade with foreign Nations shall be revived on terms of mutual advantage and goodwill, and while undertaking the organisation of the Nation's trade, import and export, it shall be the duty of the Republic of Ireland to prevent the shipment from Ireland of food and other necessaries until the wants of the Irish people are fully satisfied and the future provided for.

It shall also devolve upon the National Government to seek co-operation of the Governments of other countries in determining a standard of Social and Industrial Legislation with a view to a general and lasting improvement in the conditions under which the working classes live and labour.

Introduction

We live and work on a relatively small island in the far north-west of Europe. We are part of a global chain of commerce, movement of people and ideas. Most of us speak a language that is spoken daily by at least another 400 million persons across the globe. Our future is tied up with that of our neighbouring island as well as those countries that currently make up the European Union.[2] Yet many of the challenges we face are truly global, from the obvious effects of climate change to the less obvious effects of Brexit and the many political conflicts and humanitarian disasters that appear on our doorstep.

This book about how Ireland can be transformed by a new democratic programme. It is is for the general reader as well for trade union members. The trade union movement accounts for over 700,000 members across the island of Ireland and proudly traces its history to a time when labour asserted its rights and dignity against the dominance of capital. Our goal is to persuade and win support for a radically different society which is not only possible but desirable and achievable in this century.

This book is about the future of Ireland – its economy and society and its people. It sets out a vision for the whole of Ireland that goes beyond sectarian or political agendas. But is a vision enough? What we need is a credible and carefully worked out strategy to move towards a shared vision, a strategy currently lacking in the market for ideas and contest of programmes. Referring to different models of economic, social and political development in the recent past or abroad may be helpful but what worked then or elsewhere may not work so well now or here. We do not need a blueprint for the future because we cannot know what events and surprises await us. What we do need is a set of pointers to guide the direction of policy, action and public conversation.

One hundred years ago this year, a brave new Ireland was imagined by men and women in a gathering of elected representatives in what was the first meeting of the First Dáil or parliament on 21 January 1919 in Dublin. The Democratic Programme, which was endorsed at that meeting, was a radical document founded on the principles of equality, justice and self-determination. An earlier version drawn up by Tom Johnson, leader of the Irish Labour Party and Trade Union Congress, with the assistance of Cathal O'Shannon and William O'Brien of the Irish Transport and General Workers' Union, envisaged workers' control of industry and 'the elimination of the class in society which lives upon the wealth produced by the workers of the nation but gives no useful service in return'. This version was submitted by Johnson on the eve of the first meeting of the Dáil to an organising committee. The document was significantly adjusted, and the socialist content diluted to remove references to objectives such as the elimination of the capitalist class and workers' control. It appears that the re-editing was done by the late Seán T. O'Ceallaigh TD, who later became President of Ireland. The revised document was read out in Irish as *Clár Oibre Poblacánaighe* (Working Programme of the Republic of Ireland) on the afternoon of the following day when the First Dáil met (Daly, 2017).

Even in its edited version, the revised Democratic Programme contained many important ideas and aspirations which, if they had been acted on, would have produced a very different Ireland to the one that we know today. Failure to implement these ideas reinforced an unequal society where fundamental human rights were not honoured and where private property and class interests prevailed over the common good.

We must remember that the Democratic Programme was drafted in a revolutionary world traumatised by World War I and against a background of gathering conflict and sectarian division in Ireland. Not only was it one of the founding documents agreed at the first meeting of the Dáil, it was also the basis for an appeal for support for Irish independence by leading Irish trade unionists at the international socialist movement gathered in Berne, Switzerland in February of 1919.

What emerged following the events of 1916–22 was a bitterly divided country and the establishment of socially conservative administrations in Northern Ireland and in the Irish Free State. Failure to implement radical social change as well as to establish a strong native industrial sector in what was to become the Republic of Ireland delayed the economic transformation that could have happened much earlier and, in a way, that better vindicated fundamental human rights. In large part, the Democratic Programme remained an aspiration rather than a programme of action to transform society.

In the recent past, the inherent weaknesses in native Irish capitalism have been exposed. We have emerged from a bruising experience of recession, banking collapse and reduced living standards. While many have benefited from a recovery in employment and wages, others remain mired in poverty and precarious work.

With Brexit, all bets are off when it comes to the future of economic and political relationships within and between the islands of Ireland and Great Britain. The Belfast Agreement[3] of 1998 is under threat. The all-island economy – fragile as it has been – is precarious, with Northern Ireland particularly vulnerable. Austerity has not gone away and the slow erosion of its manufacturing base has chipped away at community morale.

Three times in my lifetime, so far, a boom in incomes, prices and living standards has been followed by a major downturn. The consequences were devastating for many hundreds of thousands of people forced to subsist on poverty incomes or seek work abroad. The choice from here on is not between 'stability' on the one hand and 'chaos' on the other but between continuing with the same policies that have characterised

Ireland over the last fifty years or taking a radically different direction based on lessons learned from other small Northern European societies.

We must find an 'Irish way' that breaks free of the shackles of overdependence on foreign capital and no longer models itself on the neo-liberal approach which has seen an erosion in equality, public service and labour rights. In particular, the model of social and economic development in Northern Ireland is not sufficient to raise standards of living, redistribute wealth and heal the wounds of sectarian conflict over many generations. We need a new departure.

Had the Republic of Ireland adopted a Norwegian approach to natural resources it could have harnessed these resources and built a strong economic position apart from the EU as Norway did from the 1970s onwards. But it is far from certain that the potential of gas and oil finds up to the present time would have provided a sufficient buffer for the Republic of Ireland to survive outside the EU. We would have needed an alternative model or strategy that was not available then and is unlikely to emerge any time soon.

We must look forward in decades and not just a few years to the next political event or election. Let us cast the net out to the middle of the century: only 30 years away, short enough to permit us to mark out a realistic strategy and vision within a manageable time scale roughly equivalent to a generation and long enough to allow for the necessary sea change in political and institutional culture.

Although this book focuses on social and economic change within Ireland, we should not forget the importance of solidarity at a global level. Climate change, poverty, migration and human rights concern everyone around the world. Ireland is in the top group of countries in terms of gross domestic product (GDP) per capita, giving us a moral duty to show leadership and initiative in promoting human and labour rights, fair trade, investment and overseas aid.

We need to change the language and thinking around 'economic growth'. What matters is sustainable human development across a range of domains encompassing nutrition, health, education and work. Growth, captured in a narrow statistical concept such as GDP, must become a *secondary* public policy goal subservient to other measures that reflect the quality of economic activity. In the first, discarded draft of the Democratic Programme, Johnson wrote: 'The Irish Republic shall always count its wealth and prosperity by the measure of health and happiness of its citizens.' If only this sentence has been left in! And if only social policy in the following decades put as much emphasis on promoting and measuring health and happiness as on GDP.

We have no clear idea of how the world will look beyond 2020 – although we can assume that it will be hotter on average, especially if the limited and under-ambitious climate change targets are further undermined by the new politics of the US. What we can be sure of is that there will be further recessions or significant slowdowns and that the environmental and social pressure of millions escaping war, terror, droughts, famines and persecution will not abate but increase.

Populist and far-right forces can build all the hard borders, walls and controls they like but nothing will stop those desperate enough to risk their lives aboard flimsy boats in rough seas or locked up in containers. They have nothing to lose, just like the millions of Europeans – including many Irish – during the eighteenth and nineteenth century who made the hazardous journey by sea to the New World. Well-managed migration is of benefit to a host country generating diversity, dissemination of new ideas and social innovation.

This book is divided into three parts and ten chapters, starting with an analysis of what can be learned from recent Irish economic history. From there, in Part II, I outline a vision for Ireland as part of a Europe in transition. Part III suggests new ideas and approaches resulting from a long overdue debate. The reader is invited to contribute to this debate with friends, colleagues and family members.

2/x/21

PART I

HOW WE GOT HERE

1

Why the Model Failed

The story as it unfolded over the last century

Those who do not learn from the past are doomed to repeat it, as Winston Churchill once said. Although partition in 1922 marked out two separate jurisdictions, it did little to help economic development. Excessive external dependence and the lack of a vibrant domestic political and economic culture left the entire island in a position of peripheral vulnerability, dogged by sectarian politics in Northern Ireland and the lack of a progressive social vision in the Irish Free State. In the years following partition, the Democratic Programme of 1919 remained a curious tract full of pious aspirations, its commitment to the nation's children, for example, remaining largely unfulfilled even today.

Ireland minus its north-east corner in the early twentieth century had more in common with the economic landscape of the mid-nineteenth century than 2019.[4] Partition created divergent economic histories reflecting the politics of industrialisation. A vibrant and confident new economy flourished in the Republic of Ireland, driven largely by foreign direct investment in the 1960s, while Northern Ireland remained heavily UK focussed. Service industries replaced declining manufacturing industries. The period of the Troubles (1968–98) further stimulated public service growth as many external firms were reluctant to locate or invest in Northern Ireland.

In the 1930s, the new Irish Free State adopted a major focus on native manufacturing enterprise, protected behind tariff walls and supported by a network of finance, advice and supply chains. New semi-state companies drove economic activity. This process of 'enterprise behind the walls' reached its height in the 1950s. It was considered a failure by the late 1950s. Economic policy in the Republic of Ireland swung from extreme protectionism to an outward-looking strategy based on tax competition, grant-aid and preparation for entry to the European Economic Community (EEC). Membership of the EEC in 1973 for both parts of the island marked a moment as historic and significant as the decision by the United Kingdom (UK) in 2016, to leave the European Union.

The dismantling of many features of the Western European post-war settlement from 1980 onwards – first in the UK and then gradually across what was then the European Community – represented another important moment with far-reaching consequences. Gone or substantially diminished in the UK were a range of post-war attainments, including protection for labour, universal social goods free at the point of use and the existence of a significant commercial state enterprise economy encompassing key utilities and parts of banking and manufacturing. Added to these trends was an almost universal dismantling of many of the regulatory controls on banking as well as restrictions on international capital flows in the name of free movement of finance capital. This huge social shift in Europe, the UK and the Republic of Ireland was a profoundly regressive counter-reform with consequences that went far beyond most people's understanding or expectations in the late 1970s or early 1980s.

By the beginning of this century the Republic of Ireland had become one of the most open economies in Europe (as measured by the relative size of imports and exports in total output). The impact of the recession of 2008 was modified by the relative strength of existing and new inward investment. The construction sector, along with retail, were the first to suffer the initial shock.

The problem then was not the foreign multinational sector itself but the weakness of the domestic sector to sufficiently take advantage of the 'green shoots' of growth from 2013 onwards. Moreover, the continuing reliance on foreign investment before, during and after the recession does not constitute a sustainable plan.

While the success of the Republic of Ireland's economy can be credited to international factors, internal policy choices have also made a difference (Healy and Slowey, 2006). Not least of significance in this mix was the success of sustained investment in the secondary and tertiary levels of education in the period 1968–2000, which laid many of the foundations for future economic success. This looked very appealing until the crash of 2008. So appealing was it, in fact, that many of the European Union new accession states, which joined the EU in 2004, sent delegations of academics and public servants to study the success of the Irish model.

Prior to 2008 the Republic of Ireland was formally compliant with EU fiscal rules in relation to the government deficit and the overall level of debt. Public expenditure did increase rapidly, but from what had been a low base. In the run-up to the crash of 2008 the Economic and Social Research Institute (ESRI) published two landmark books entitled *Bust to Boom: the Irish Experience of Growth and Inequality* (2000) and *Best of Times? The Social Impact of the Celtic Tiger* (2007). Concerns were signalled by some economists, including those at the ESRI, that a large asset bubble was forming and would not last. Even so, the term 'soft landing' was invoked as the most probable outcome once growth slowed down. Nobody could have predicted such a sharp decline in GDP, a rapid and catastrophic collapse in the Irish banking system and an escalating fiscal crisis as revenues stopped or slowed down. It was a perfect storm and in a matter of months the Republic of Ireland went from being a poster child of liberal economic policies to a complete economic failure where, by 2010, international lenders no longer had any confidence in Irish financial institutions or in the solvency of the Irish sovereign. This followed the sovereign's socialisation of an enormous amount of private debt, much of it ultimately foreign related. The intervention of the Troika (the European Commission, the European Central Bank and the International Monetary Fund) in late 2010 paved the way for prolongation of fiscal austerity and many problematic social reforms.

The Republic of Ireland recovered gradually from 2012, due in no small part to the buoyant nature of the foreign sector as well as more benign conditions in global markets. However, the pace of economic recovery was driven by a slow recovery in demand and employment in the large domestic economy. A significant facilitating factor in global and therefore Irish economic recovery was the positive role of UK and US administrations in undertaking monetary and fiscal stabilisation measures in the earliest years of the economic downturn (mainly in 2009 and 2010). A gradual return in capital market confidence in Irish sovereign bond issues was helped by large-scale purchases by the extraordinarily influential fund manager Michael Hasenstab in the summer of 2011. He took a huge risk on low-value Irish government bonds on the secondary markets and it paid back handsomely some years later.

It is misleading to claim that the whole of the Republic of Ireland was living beyond its means in the years leading up to the crisis of 2008. The public sector was close to balance in the years prior to the crash and went into significant deficit only after the economic collapse. The Irish balance sheet recession was amplified, for a time, by excessive fiscal austerity and an expenditure-loaded fiscal austerity strategy.[5]

The impact of recession in Northern Ireland was less severe than in the Republic of Ireland. There was a particular spillover from the sharp downturn in construction on both sides of the border. The overall impact of the global recession was less partly due to UK-wide considerations including stimulus spending and monetary easing.[6] Also, the strength of public spending and employment in Northern Ireland provided a certain buffer against the adverse effects of a collapse in external and internal demand. Nevertheless, the collapse in construction activity did have particularly adverse spillover impacts in Northern Ireland as evidenced by a relatively large fall in property prices compared to other UK regions.

The economy of Northern Ireland remains embedded in a large UK market where it avails of economies of scale, significant fiscal transfers from the UK government and unified regulatory and pricing structures for many lines of economic activity. Its degree of integration with Great Britain is much stronger, economically, than is the case with the Republic of Ireland, although particular sectors such as agri-food – as well as small and medium-sized enterprises (SMEs) – are relatively more integrated in the all-island economy of Ireland. In common with northern regions of the UK, Northern Ireland suffered a deficit in productivity only partially ameliorated by fiscal transfers that reduced the gap in living standards across the UK.

David Begg (2016, p. 202) reminds us that, 'In the 90 years or so since independence Ireland has looked into the abyss of economic destruction four times.' It is unlikely that there will be only *four* such occasions: we have yet to encounter the fifth abyss. The one constant theme in recent Irish economic history is that of external over-reliance coupled with a weak internal and domestically owned enterprise base.

An overdependence on external support

A large-scale dependence on inward investment and export share, especially in leading sectors such as pharmaceuticals and IT services, leaves the economy highly exposed to sudden downturns or medium-term trends in investment location.

A noticeable feature of economic development in both parts of Ireland has been a consistent failure by domestically owned enterprises to seize a commanding position in generating economic growth, innovation and export performance. The result has been a lopsided reliance on foreign direct investment in the case of the Republic of Ireland and, in the case of Northern Ireland, a high dependence on public service employment and direct financial contributions from the UK government. Some foreign direct investment activity – particularly in the Republic of Ireland – has involved a high degree of 're-exporting' where companies buy most of their inputs from abroad (frequently other branches or subsidiaries of the same international company) and then export the bulk of what is produced. In these cases, there is often a limited linkage to local producer supply chains.

Nevertheless, large-scale inward investment by foreign multinationals has brought a welcome flow of additional investment and revenue as well as income and employment. Continuation of such investment is highly dependent on the medium-term location decisions of large multinational companies. But while some manufacturing plants and IT services are here for the foreseeable future, we cannot be sure how developments such as Brexit, for example, will impact on location decisions of some major international players.

US tax policy as well as continuing pressure in the EU for a common consolidated tax base (CCTB) indicates that the opposition by the Irish government and some other EU member states to reform in this area is not tenable. CCTB is a proposal to create a single set of rules to calculate corporate tax liability across member states. The strong preference of many EU states is to base tax liability on where profits and sales accrue. The proposal for an EU digital tax envisages that profits of digital companies are taxed where revenues accrue rather than where profits are booked for the purposes of avoiding the payment of corporate tax.

Indeed, a bargain may yet be sought on EU support for Ireland on the detail of a long-term Brexit transition in return for greater flexibility on CCTB, support for an EU digital tax and related matters. There is also a long-term reputational concern for governments to work together to regulate corporate activities and ensure that multinationals are not taking advantage of loopholes or targeted tax measures to relocate parts of their activity in various parts of the world. The use of such measures as 'knowledge boxes'[7] are dubious in this respect.

Up to now, Irish governments have hidden behind the Organisation for Economic Cooperation and Development (OECD) and argued that progress on a CCTB is not desirable until a more global intercontinental agreement on tax is put in place. The OECD base erosion and profit shifting (BEPS)[8] process is a slow start in the right direction. However, both OECD and the US have signalled the possibility of a consensus in 2020. This marks trouble for the traditional Irish corporate strategy.

It is clear from an examination of various national accounts released by the Central Statistics Office (CSO) that the position of multinational companies is a significant explanatory factor in the huge share of corporate profits in total national income. While a significant part of the profits earned in the Republic of Ireland by foreign-based enterprises are 'repatriated', the rest remains in the state either as retained earnings or funds used for reinvestment and distribution. It is no exaggeration to state that there are, in reality, two economies in the Republic of Ireland: a high-productivity, low labour-intensive, export-orientated and highly profitable economy on the one hand, and a relatively low-productivity, high labour-intensive, domestically oriented and, in some cases, relatively less profitable economy on the other.

The closest the CSO can come to publishing relevant aggregate data on these two economies is under the headings of Foreign Sector and Domestic Dominated Sectors (CSO, 2018a). Included in the foreign sector are pharma, information and communications technology (ICT) and similar sectors. By 2015–16, the Foreign Sector accounted for close to 40 per cent of total gross value added (GVA). It is likely that a small number of enterprises account for around 40 per cent of total GVA and 50 per cent of gross operating surplus (similar to corporate profits). The CSO, Department of Finance (2018) and Revenue Commissioners indicate high degrees of output concentration with implications for corporation tax receipts. The Department of Finance analysis showed that, in manufacturing, the top 10 per cent of enterprises accounted for close to 90 per cent of value added and over 70 per cent of employment in the period 2006–14. Output and employment are more concentrated in the Republic of Ireland than in other OECD countries for which comparable data are available.

During the recession of 2008 the larger foreign sector enterprises saw little or no decline in output or production apart from a relatively small dip in 2008 and again in 2013 (CSO, 2018a). This explains the relative stability of wages in firms and sectors associated with the foreign sector. The story in the rest of the economy is very different where job losses, wage cuts and recruitment freezes were the order of the day.[9] Outside the business economy, the public service fell to the ravages of wage cuts, programme cuts and voluntary staff departures.

The potential for statistical distortion is well recognised, especially in light of the surge in measured GDP and some of its main components in 2015. *Productivity in Ireland, 2016* (CSO, 2018a) provides useful insights into the distribution of productivity by economic sector and type of enterprise ownership in the period 2000–16.[10] There is a marked difference in productivity performance between foreign-owned and Irish-owned manufacturing enterprises. Productivity in Irish-owned firms is above native-owned firms in most other EU countries (Figure 1). However, whether measured on productivity, innovation or export share, most domestic businesses struggle to compete on global markets.

The rate of business enterprise start-up is low in the Republic of Ireland compared to other EU member states. The relative position of the Republic is better regarding business survival. On a different metric, the rate of patent applications for the Republic fared reasonably well by EU standards in 2014, although the Irish data should be treated with caution given the complexities of classification of intellectual property in companies locating in Ireland.[11]

Multinationals have long operated 'transfer pricing' to book their profits in the Republic of Ireland to avail of lower corporate tax rates. One outcome of this has been an exceptionally high gap between GDP and gross national income (GNI) after repatriation of profits has been calculated. Recently, there has been a rise in relocation decisions regarding intellectual property by a small number of key players. Together with highly profitable aircraft leasing and estimates for depreciation of intellectual assets, GDP and some of its components has behaved erratically since 2015. It has been dubbed 'leprechaun economics' (Figure 2). Much of national income – no matter how it is measured (GDP, GNI or modified GNI labelled GNI*) – is reliant on the economic activity of large enterprises liable to relocate in response to cost or tax changes. These businesses may not all be footloose immediately but are potentially so in the long term.

A pattern of misallocated investment

If investment, innovation and growth in the foreign and domestic sectors have been lopsided, it is noticeable that investment in the latter sector has been historically weighted towards questionable lines of return. Property-related investment in the Republic of Ireland has been 'pro-cyclical' – rising as a percentage of GDP when GDP was growing rapidly and falling when GDP contracted or grows more slowly. Much of the surge in capital investment in the 1998–2007 period was construction-related and highly speculative. And the nature of this misallocation only became fully apparent with the emergence of unfinished ghost estates, empty shopping centres and hotels, often in places far removed from transport hubs and vital community services.

The misallocation of capital to speculative investment before the 2008 recession was associated with typically low levels of investment by domestic enterprises in productive assets – a point stressed by Ó Riain (2014, p. 70).[12] While mistakes were made before the Celtic Tiger years, it is important to note that these were compounded from the mid-1990s onwards and especially in the years before the 2008 crash. More than one Celtic Tiger sub-period has been identified in the 1987–2007 period.[13]

The nature of economic growth changed around the time of the new millennium. Rapid export growth and investment in productive capital increasingly gave way to a credit-fuelled domestic consumption boom with a particularly fast growth in construction.[14]

Rossa White (2010) shows that a disproportionate amount of capital investment in the years immediately prior to 2008 went towards housing stock and other forms of property while productive investment was led mainly by state or EU investment as well as foreign private capital. The reduction in the rate of capital gains tax from 40 to 20 per cent in 1998 was a factor in stimulating investment – but in some cases in the wrong type of capital.[15] Allied to this tax cut was a boom in risky lending, which exposed private banks to the crash in 2008.

Coupled with other tax reliefs such as 'Section 23' property relief, the measures adopted in the years immediately prior to 2008 added fuel to the fire with the result that there was over-investment in the wrong type of property in the wrong places. Total credit for construction and real estate grew rapidly. Real estate and construction accounted for 22 per cent of total outstanding loan amounts in March 2008 (firms and households). The outstanding loans to these sectors represented 46 per cent of the credit extended to Irish resident firms (Central Bank of Ireland, 2015).

Indigenous enterprise and corporate culture

A toxic relationship involving land and property, risky forms of banking and risky lending had already been well established by the time the crisis hit in 2008. Regling and Watson (2010, pp. 34–35) in their account of the sources of Ireland's banking collapse in 2008–9 spoke of 'a collective governance failure ... an uncritical enthusiasm for property acquisition that became something of a national blind-spot.' Speaking to the Institute of Bankers in Ireland in November 2006, Brian Cowen, Minister for Finance at the time, explained:

> But in my view it is the innovation coming from within the sector which is the most remarkable driver of change. Increasingly sophisticated derivative products seem to be arriving daily as the sector seeks to become ever more professional in the way it manages and hedges its risks and chases after that elusive 'higher' yield. Of course, not all of these brave new initiatives are successful. It's a hard game, but there's all to play for. Of course that's easy for me to say because you are players on the field and I'm just an ardent supporter on the sidelines. I will continue to wear your colours.[16]

Given the direction of policy in the preceding years, the 2008 banking and property crash was unavoidable – the degree of its severity was simply a question of timing. Nearly all analysts apart from a handful of contrarians hugely under-projected the scale of collapse in asset prices, confidence and investment. Too many economists had bought into the notion of the 'efficient markets hypothesis' where financial markets, left to themselves, would find the right price level. Former USA Secretary to the Treasury, Timothy Geithner, nailed it in an interview with *The Financial Times* in 2014:

> Our crisis was largely a failure of imagination. Every crisis is. For all my talk about tail risk we didn't foresee how a nationwide decline in home prices could induce panic ... I got to see how much power the belief in the 'Great Moderation' had over smart people ... the widespread belief that devastating financial crises were a thing of the past.

The development of complex financial products and instruments in recent decades above and below the radar of financial regulation has generated a thriving industry of vast sums of money changing hands. Alongside it a huge level of private debt has been created with a complex allocation of repackaged tranches of risky assets in the form of products such as collateralised debt obligations, heavily promoted as yielding high rates of return to the assets' owners. When the asset price bubble burst in the US in 2007 there was an international chain reaction as the bottom fell out of the sub-prime markets and ripple effects spread through the entire complex, inter-connected and highly globalised finance system. From the start of the counter-revolution in 1980 the ratio of financial asset values to GDP for the world as a whole rose sharply (Palma, 2009). If total world GDP was around $60 trillion dollars in 2007, total financial assets were over $300 trillion. To put this in perspective, the entire GDP of the European Union economy was just short of €20 trillion in 2019.

It is difficult to know, at any time, who owns what because bonds issued or held by corporate actors are beyond the reach and knowledge of society including, most worryingly, financial regulators. When a bondholder is said to be burned it is impossible to tell which financial intermediaries and, ultimately, which households are most impacted: the mediation between equity, loans, dividends, royalties and various revenue streams and capital gains and losses is fiendishly complex.

Traditional retail banking where savers (businesses or individuals) deposited money and borrowers took out a loan to buy a house, a car or an education was compromised in the period prior to 2008. The lessons of the 1920s and 1930s had been forgotten or ignored along with the legal and regulatory measures adopted in the wake of the Great Depression of 1929. This was exemplified by the enactment of the Glass-Steagall legislation in the US in 1933. A key component of this legislation was the separation of retail from investment (or what is sometimes termed as casino banking). Following pressures from vested interests, the Gramm-Leach-Bliley Act of 1999 with bipartisan political support in the US repealed much of the Glass-Steagall provisions just in time for a nasty partial repeat performance of the collapse of 1929. The roots of the 2008–10 crash are complex and varied but included a trend towards de-regulation of which the 1999 Act is an example.

The international dismantling of financial regulations from the 1980s onwards also paved the way for financial instability. The Minsky moment – named after Hyman Minsky (1919–96) – is an acknowledgement of financial instability born out of an exuberance of markets and the short-term accumulation of private corporate debt. Many politicians and analysts believe that the crash of 2008 will not happen again – at least not as severely as before. However, a Minsky moment arrives every few decades. Irish capitalism, with its newfound wealth, debt and global financial linkages is especially vulnerable. It used to be said that when the UK caught a cold, Ireland caught pneumonia. These days it is surely the case that when the advanced economies of Europe and the US catch a cold, the Republic of Ireland catches an advanced form of pleurisy!

The flip side of the crash was shown when global conditions improved, as they did after 2013. The Republic of Ireland bounced back and moved forward much faster than other Eurozone economies, taking advantage of global conditions, corporate investment decisions, including tax-planning initiatives and under-utilised capacity in the domestic economy. Meanwhile, Northern Ireland suffered disproportionately from the downturn in construction activity (mirroring the all-island nature of that sector). Still, UK economists and government officials failed to see and appreciate the implications of financialisation for economic stability[17].

In other words, the excesses of the Celtic Tiger (some of which spilled over into Northern Ireland by way of extended credit and construction boom activity) mirrored global trends and imbalances associated with the global neo-liberal project. This observation in no way takes from the fact that domestic policy oversight and regulation were woefully absent in the years prior to the crash (and immediately after) as explained in the 2016 Oireachtas report into the banking crisis.

Sweeney (2013a, p. 94) has pointed out that a strong focus on public sector efficiency and accountability to the relative neglect of private sector corporate governance failure has character- ised public discourse in Ireland: '... it was not the public sector profligacy which caused the collapse of the Irish economy, but appalling practices in some of Ireland's leading indigenous pri- vate sector firms, including the banks.'

A corporate shareholder ethos in Anglo-American economies emphasised short-term gain over long-term vision, facilitating a growth in the 'bonus culture' with an ever-increasing disparity in earnings within enterprises and a prioritising of short-term equity holding as well as higher levels of corporate debt over long-term equity holdings.

The price of diluted sovereignty

Membership of the European Union has brought many economic benefits to the whole of Ireland, but a price has been paid in terms of domestic policy discretion. While right-leaning critics of the EU point to migration and alleged interference in business affairs, critics on the left point to the policies of fiscal austerity or neo-liberalism and interference in decisions regarding own- ership of public assets and competition. A key ingredient in the augmented crisis of 2008 was the role of European monetary policy and the dysfunctional nature of banking regulation, policy and practice across the European Union. Added to this was the nefarious role of pro-cyclical fiscal policy. In other words, public spending and taxation policies served to deepen the recession in many European countries of which the Republic of Ireland was one. Unfortunately, the institutional framework and ideological bias remains in place today.

The boom in lending for commercial and domestic property during the 'crazy' phase of the Celtic Tiger[18] was facilitated by at least two significant factors: (i) a boom in inter-bank lending involving exposure, especially by British, US, French and German banks, and (ii) positive risk assessments of financial institutions by the main rating agencies. These interlinking developments, supported and facilitated by misguided domestic economic policies, laid the ground for retribution in 2008–10 involving the collapse and insolvency of more than one bank, a huge depletion of public finances and, especially, an insistence by international creditors and nations that no corporate senior bondholder would be left behind and that some banks were too big to fail.[19] In short, the answer to a private sector banking crisis was a public sector bailout coupled with fiscal austerity to restore public finances and reassure international capital markets.

Much of the cost of bank bailouts was transferred to the people. The associated programme of austerity took its toll economically and socially. Factors not directly related to banking such as overdependence on construction or property-related taxes were also at work during this period. Some of the bailout money was returned in subsequent years by way of bank equity sales by the Irish government, but in the meantime the damage done by way of reduced incomes, job losses and depleted public services was clear to see.

A declining wage share and rising personal debt

Relative to wages, more profits are retained or re-invested or distributed to shareholders. Many wage-earning households have accumulated assets and seen a rise in various forms of non-labour income but wages still account for the bulk of household income. Among households, wages account for approximately 60 per cent of total personal gross income; state transfers (pensions or other welfare payments) account for 20 per cent; and other incomes (rent, interest, dividends etc.) make up the remaining 20 per cent. The share of wages in total national income (households and corporations combined) has been trending downwards since the mid-1990s and is now well below 50 per cent of GDP in the Republic of Ireland.

The availability of easy consumer and mortgage credit up to 2007 concealed a longer-term trend in the share of wages in income. Wage share since the 1980s has declined sharply as a proportion of total income in the Republic of Ireland while total income or production – GDP, GNI or GVA – has grown dramatically since the early 1990s. The Republic of Ireland is not unique in this respect: in other economies, notably the US and the UK, the share of wages has declined over time. The reasons for this are many and complex (see, for example, an analysis of recent trends in the Republic of Ireland by Paul Sweeney, 2013b) but include the regressive direction of public policy, the dismantling of labour protection and the rise of super profit sectors as well as the influence of globalisation, technology and financialisation.

Yet there is something odd about the extent to which wages have declined in relative terms in the Republic of Ireland. The clue lies in the multinational sector. Measuring wages as a proportion of GDP is not reliable due to transfer pricing or distorting factors such as a surge in investment under the heading of intellectual property and tax inversion strategies by large multinational corporations. A more meaningful comparison is to look at the share of household income that comes from wages[20] (Figure 3).

Wage share conforms to a cyclical as well as a long-term structural pattern, which can be confusing. During the early part of recession, the share of 'non-wages' (corporate profits, 'mixed income', farming income and other income flows) tends to fall as a percentage of total economy income while the share of wages rises, even though wages may be falling in absolute terms. During a recovery such as from 2012 onwards, profits and other forms of income rebound rapidly while the share of wages falls. These patterns are easier to discern if looking at primary household income – the income earned by households (wages, rents, dividends, etc.) before receipt of social transfers (e.g. pensions and child benefits) and before deduction of taxes on income.

The recovery in wages (whether measured in hourly, weekly or annual terms) has been modest compared to the eye-watering leaps in GDP (Figure 2). The share of wages rose up to 2009 as employment and incomes increased. After peaking in 2009 the share fell from 81 to 78 per cent by 2016. Estimates based on trends since then indicate a likely figure of 77 per cent in 2018, around where it was just before the 2008 recession.

Up to 1995 the Irish wage share as measured by GDP began to decouple from that in the US, the UK and the original fifteen EU member states. A squeeze on wages as a proportion of national income created unforeseen vulnerabilities. As in the UK and the US and alongside evidence of rising wage inequality, wage repression induced a dependence by households on debt to maintain consumption.

Notwithstanding rising labour force participation by women in recent decades, wages have not been adequate to enable couples or individuals to cover the cost of living without recourse to higher borrowing. And so borrowing rose dramatically, particularly in the years leading up to 2008. All of this coincided with lax lending rules, huge inter-country capital flows and a low interest regime within the Eurozone.

Inequality and the role of the state

International evidence points to marked differences in the extent of economic inequality across countries – even countries with similar levels of income per capita. Some countries tend to have high levels of inequality in income before taxes or social transfers are taken into account, although these even out income to some degree.[21] In the absence of taxes and transfers, rates of poverty and deprivation would be at levels typically observed in poorer parts of the globe. Were it not for social welfare payments, 45 per cent of the population would be at risk of poverty in 2016. Put another way, the level of at-risk poverty in 2016 was 16.5 per cent, indicating that social welfare prevented 28.4 per cent of the population from falling into poverty. This proportion of the population prevented from falling into poverty rose from 14 per cent points in 2001 to 28 per cent in 2016.

The variation in performance across countries shows that inequality and poverty are not inevitable. Rather, they are caused by a combination of factors, including deliberate social policies. Some political economists (and their political allies) emphasise the positive role of inequality in allowing the gifted and the hard-working to do well and to contribute to successful businesses. The implication of this thinking is that there are certain levels of acceptable inequality, which is why these economists like to shift the focus of statistical analysis away from 'relative poverty' (really a measure of income inequality) to that of deprivation or absolute poverty. It may be argued that poverty and deprivation can be abolished for all but the most extreme cases not amenable to public intervention. Acute and residual deprivation is a complex area but is often associated with particular mental health conditions. These, in turn, are associated with social inequality. Beyond that, some may argue, inequality in income and wealth is not something that governments should be overly concerned about, provided that the populace is broadly content.

But inequality matters to everyone. Copious research by, among others, Wilkinson and Pickett (2009) has documented the negative effects of inequality on health, education, social cohesion and positive civic engagement. More equal societies, such as the Scandinavian countries, tend to be healthier, happier and wealthier than other societies.

In recent years, inequality of income in the Republic of Ireland after taxes and social welfare payments are taken into account is close to midway on a ranking of countries by the percentage of disposable income going to the top 5 per cent of households (Figure 4).

On the face of this evidence, the Republic of Ireland appears to be in a good position regarding income inequality, especially compared to many other European countries. But this does not tell the full story as income taxes and cash social transfers redistribute income among households. Inequality in gross income, before taxes and welfare payments are applied to household income, is significantly high in Ireland. Figure 5 shows a measure of inequality called the Gini coefficient before and after cash social transfers for EU28 member states. Values of the Gini coefficient typically lie between 20 and 50 (where 0 would imply perfect equality of all households and 100 perfect inequality with one person or household receiving all of the income in a country).

The Republic of Ireland appears to be close to the EU average both in terms of income distribution before and after social transfers. The degree of 'lifting' to be done by social transfers (not taking account of the interaction of income taxes on distribution of income) does not appear to be unusual in the Republic of Ireland compared to other EU states. In fact Denmark, Sweden, France and Germany all have higher levels of inequality in income before the application of taxes and transfers.

Figure 6 shows trends in the Gini coefficient before and after social transfers for the Republic of Ireland over a period of thirteen years up to 2016. After peaking during the recession years (2008–12), the level of inequality has settled at a level of around 50 before transfers and just above 30 after transfers. Clearly social transfers did provide some relative protection to large sections of the population during the period of fiscal austerity. That said, levels of poverty and deprivation rose during the recession and particular household types were disproportionately affected (in particular single adult households with children). But what is most striking about Figure 6 is the extent of 'state lifting' by means of social transfers. While the Republic of Ireland does not stand out with regard to the equalising effects of social transfers, it is noticeable how the role of social transfers has become more important over time. In this case, the comparison relates to the period 2003–16, within which a major economic shock occurred that triggered temporary higher social transfers. Additionally, the role of social transfers is likely to increase as our population ages, posing significant challenges for taxation and pensions policies.

The CSO adjusts for the composition of households by estimating equivalised disposable income per individual. The average or median figure was €20,597 in 2016. The poverty threshold (where someone is at risk of poverty) is taken as 60 per cent of this median value, €12,227. A narrower definition of poverty is what is referred to as 'consistent poverty', which is measured with reference to those at risk of poverty and at the same time experiencing enforced deprivation in two or more dimensions.[22] Just over 8 per cent of all individuals experienced deprivation in 2016. Under half of those in consistent poverty reported going without heating at some stage in the previous twelve months.

Many of those in consistent poverty were children, lone parents, the unemployed and low-paid workers. Of those in paid work, 1.9 per cent were in consistent poverty and 12.6 per cent experienced deprivation.

Healy, Bourke, Leahy, Murphy, Murphy and Reynolds (2016) have drawn attention to a pattern of worsening income distribution before and after transfers in the immediate aftermath of the fiscal crisis in 2008–12 with higher levels of deprivation among those at work. The top two income deciles increased their share of (equivalised) disposable income while the bottom two deciles experienced the biggest fall in the period 2008–14. The recession affected almost everyone but those least able to manage were affected the most. And when the value of 'social goods' (health, education, social care) was considered, the likely hit for the very poorest was greater.

These indicators suggest rising inequality over time in direct income from work or capital, increasing pressure on the government to redistribute income through the tax and welfare systems, making it ever more difficult to sustain this level of redistribution through the tax and social welfare code.

A direct statistical comparison of Northern Ireland and the Republic of Ireland is not possible as different measures and definitions of poverty are used. The data show a pattern of stability in relative income inequality with a spike during the years of recession (Figure 8). If the Northern Ireland economy were to undergo a new downturn it is very likely that poverty rates would rise significantly.

The Republic of Ireland is characterised by a high degree of wage inequality as evidenced by international comparisons furnished by the OECD. In 2016 over one in five full-time workers earned less than two thirds of median earnings – the benchmark typically used to identify low-paid workers (Figure 9). This proportion was significantly higher than in most other European countries. France, Switzerland, Italy, Denmark and Finland have much more compressed wage spreads than the Republic of Ireland.

Wealth is more unequally distributed than income, yet the focus of analysis, policy debate and available statistical information is on income. The CSO recently undertook a statistical survey of wealth in the Republic of Ireland (CSO, 2015a). This survey reports data on housing, land, investments, valuables, savings and private occupational pensions and nets out any borrowings (mortgages, loans, credit card debt) to give a measure of net wealth (Figure 10). Lawless and Lynch (2016) provide some estimates:

- The bottom 20 per cent of households (ranked by net wealth) had no positive net wealth; they owe more than they own.
- The top 10 per cent of households owned an estimated 54 per cent of all net wealth.
- The top 5 per cent owned an estimated 38 per cent of all net wealth.[23]
- The top 1 per cent owned 14 per cent of all net wealth.[24]

Research by economists of the Central Bank of Ireland shows a more unequal distribution of wealth compared to the rest of the Eurozone but much less unequal compared to the US.[25]

Three points emerge from an analysis of data on personal wealth in the Republic of Ireland: (i) Wealth (net of debt) is unequally distributed in the Republic with the top 10 per cent of households owning over half of the total; (ii) Inequality of wealth, although not as severe as the US, is somewhat greater in the Republic of Ireland than across the Eurozone countries; and (iii) Inequality in wealth has increased since the 1980s, reflecting a mix of factors including demography, tax policy and house prices.

In summary, the picture regarding inequality is complex and the role of the state through its spending and service programmes is not well understood. There is much focus on cash transfers but, while these are extremely important in redistributing income, they are only part of the overall picture of inequality.

An unbalanced structure of government revenue

Inequality of outcomes is related to many factors including how much government raises in taxation. Government revenue in the Republic of Ireland is low as a proportion of national income. Moreover, the share of revenue from employer social contributions is very low by EU norms. International comparisons based on GDP are misleading to the extent that Irish GDP is inflated by the presence of tax-avoiding multinational activity that has limited relevance and connection to the rest of the Irish economy. That said, such activities do fall within the scope of GDP as defined by international organisations and remain taxable by national authorities. Moreover, GDP remains the relevant benchmark for the purposes of measuring compliance with EU fiscal rules on debt and deficits. There is no ideal solution to the problem of measuring wealth or income in Ireland given these distortions, but an approach taken by Goldrick-Kelly and McDonnell (2017) is useful because it compares countries at similar levels of economic development on the basis of revenue per capita. Their research shows systematic under-taxing in the Irish economy relative to social needs in the areas of childcare, education, public transport, housing and health (though spending could be more efficient, especially in the case of the latter).

Low- to mid-income workers pay relatively little in income tax, to the surprise of many when presented with the comparative data. The Republic of Ireland has a relatively poor 'social wage' as measured by access to public goods such as health, childcare and public transport. Yet wage inequality is high by OECD norms. Putting these facts together casts light on why the Irish government relies heavily on tax reliefs for lower-income households and social transfers to avoid what would otherwise be a socially unacceptable outcome in terms of poverty and inequality. Employers pay relatively little but so do workers in terms of personal income. The shortfall in public spending is plugged by means of indirect taxes. The consequences of privitising pensions, as well as the costs of housing, healthcare and education, is that many people will face high levels of financial debt or risk of poverty, especially later in life. An example of this relates to people in the private rental market, who may never have owned a home, and who will not be able to afford private rent on a modest pension. They are likely to worry about making ends meet not just when starting a family but also in the longer term, when facing retirement and the risks of sickness associated with old age.

During the boom years the Republic of Ireland witnessed a pattern of declining average income tax rates for all income bands combined with modest increases in inequality and restricted public services. Even with the recent surge in GDP there is a continuing crisis in key public services from mental health services to childcare and eldercare.

An over-reliance on revenues that rise and fall with economic activity, especially under the heading of corporation taxes, ensures that the Republic of Ireland remains hugely exposed to a potential revenue shock – as happened in 2008. The same could happen again were there to be a sudden pause in international trade or inward investment.

Divergence and convergence

GDP statistics can be misleading: trends in GPD per capita, for
example, sit uneasily with a household sentiment of being worse
off. There are complex issues of distribution within and across
households as well as areas of comparison that are difficult due to
the choice of social services over cash income in many European
countries. One way to compare countries is to use a measure
known as actual individual consumption (AIC).

AIC provides a better measure of living standards than GDP
per capita especially in comparisons involving the Republic of
Ireland. The term AIC is misleading because it seems to have little
to do with the notion of collective goods and services (including
publicly provided goods and services 'consumed' by individuals
such as public housing, public transport, public health and public
education). AIC encompasses those goods and services to which
people have access by virtue of their own income or wages as well
as those goods and services provided collectively by society. There
is a sharp contrast between GDP per capita as a measure of total
income and what is referred to by Eurostat as AIC.

Figure 11 shows the contrast in country ranking for the
Republic of Ireland: on a measure such as GDP per capita it was
the second highest in the EU after Luxembourg. However, the
latter has a rather average level of living standards as proxied by
real actual individual consumption per capita. It is below the
average for either the EU28 and EU15 (the fifteen member states
before 2004). In 2017 the Republic of Ireland was at a level of 82
per cent of average living standards in the UK as a whole.[26]

So, while cash personal income and GDP and GVA per capita
are all significantly higher in the Republic of Ireland compared
to Northern Ireland, the total consumption of households based
on consumption of public health and education services as well
as personal consumption is probably about the same, prompting
the possibly surprising conclusion that there is a rough parity of
living standards on the island of Ireland.

Key weaknesses in the Irish models

The features that mark out both parts of Ireland in the early twenty-first century include strongly positive demographics and skills (especially in the Republic of Ireland); strong trade and investment links with the US and Britain; a stable political environment, even if characterised by a certain continuing paralysis in Northern Ireland; and the persistence of imbalance in both economies, with the Republic heavily dependent on inward investment and Northern Ireland on public services to sustain existing living standards.

The economy of the Republic of Ireland is characterised by a number of key deficiencies at the root of periodic crises. Some of these weaknesses, though not all, are also apparent in the case of Northern Ireland. They include:

- an under-developed indigenous enterprise sector coupled with excessive reliance on global capital;
- the misallocation of investment typified by excessive lending to commercial property interests in the years leading up to 2008;
- partial loss of sovereignty exemplified by the preponderance of cheap money on foot of low interest rates in the Eurozone and the removal of capital controls and regulatory checks;
- weak compliance with whatever financial regulatory checks were in place before 2008;
- an imbalanced structure of public revenue with a heavy reliance on taxes from property transactions and corporate taxes as well as a hugely exposed public finance position once incomes, consumption and profits fall;
- rising wage and market income inequality during the boom period offset by a lopsided tax structure that subsidised low pay through low employer social insurance and the removal of low-paid workers from the personal income tax net.

Put simpler, many low-paid workers do not pay income tax but, in return, get a poor level of public services so that the bargain seems to be one of paying less income tax in exchange for a higher bill for education, health and other public goods. The same applies to higher paid workers.

Learning the lessons

The Celtic Tiger was not just an aberration from which we have learned our salutary lesson, never to happen again because we have taken the necessary actions. That 'all right to private property must be subordinated to the public right and welfare' as stated in the Democratic Programme a century ago has not been the case is well illustrated by recent economic history. The deadly combination of a love affair with property ownership, corruption in banking, a dedication to the rights of private property and land over all else as well as the linkages between economic power, politics and social class privilege set the scene for the last crash – and yet the seeds of the next one may already be sown.

The causes of the recent economic malaise go beyond failures in corporate and public governance and relate to the fundamental choices and values at the heart of political economy. There was a broad consensus in the Republic of Ireland, which saw the new order of deregulation or light-touch regulation from banking to planning as both desirable and unavoidable in a fast-changing and competitive world. It was assumed that everyone could be better off by paying lower taxes and by purchasing their own home, education and future pension on the basis of a share in finance capitalism. Rates of lending facilitated by exceptionally low interest rates and systematic tax reliefs and reductions in headline taxes from the late 1990s helped create the tragedy of the Celtic Tiger.

The failure of banking to serve the public interest was a major revelation of the recent crisis. Yet, a lack of open competition and a withdrawal of state equity holdings in the major financial institutions indicates that other options have not been seriously considered, including a more diversified and localised public banking system such as is in Germany.

This chapter traces some of the recent history of economic development on the island of Ireland. It suggests a weak level of ✓ indigenous development as well as a disproportionate reliance on foreign direct investment. While EU membership, among other factors, has been important for growth in productivity and living standards, it can restrict the capacity to follow an independent monetary, fiscal and social policy. However, being in the EU does not prevent us from also adopting at least some of the features of Nordic countries that are also EU members. If any lessons can be learned from recent decades it is that we need to invest in a much stronger indigenous sector and strike a better balance between ✓ public services, wages and taxes. Because, ultimately, we get what we pay for.

2

Three Big Ideas to Change Ireland: Democracy, Equality and Sustainability

Three big ideas – democracy, equality and sustainability – may serve to challenge and refocus debate in a different direction.

The terms democracy and equality are frequently used in public discourse in a narrow legal or institutional sense. So, for example, democracy is understood to apply to a process of deliberation every few years in which citizens with the right to vote can do so based on a competition by political parties. Those elected to govern are said to have a mandate to make decisions, enact new laws and authorise policies and actions over a number of years. Likewise, the term equality is used to refer to the formal equality of persons before the law and the conferring of rights to citizenship and to vote. At most, consideration is given to equality of opportunity but rarely is equality of access to power, to wealth and to media considered extensively. Even less consideration is given to equality of access to love, care and solidarity – matters that impact on all groups in society including migrants, sexual minorities or vulnerable children and the elderly. As Baker, Lynch, Cantillon and Walsh point out (2009, p. 137), 'relations of love, care and solidarity help to establish a basic sense of importance, value and belonging, a sense of being appreciated, wanted and cared about'.

That economic inequality is at unacceptably high levels and increasing in some parts of the world raises a challenge for us in seeking a more just society. Inequality breeds discontent and a breakdown in social cohesion, to which the response may be a right-wing, racist and even violent one, blaming the wrong people and offering the wrong reasons for a sense of acute unfairness and exclusion: yet, paradoxically, inequality can be the spur to a renewed, popular programme of support for pro-equality policies and institutions.

Sustainability is often associated by consumers with recycling, switching energy providers and being generally kinder to the environment. But sustainability is much more than this: it is about rethinking and revisiting our inter-generational covenant. We do not inherit the earth from our parents but borrow it from our children. Political economy has a vital role to play in helping shape such a vision. Fundamental to economic and social progress, as correctly understood by those who framed the 1919 Democratic Programme, is the role of ownership and control of resources, decision-making institutions and the values shaping these.

Time for a real democratic revolution

The concept of democracy is often applied to the practice of parliamentary democracy, yet the idea of democracy, which comes from the Greek words *demos* (people) and *kratos* (power), extends beyond the formal political or legal institutions of society. Democracy as an idea extends into civic organisations as well as enterprises where *kratos* is widely dispersed among the *demos*. The notion of distributed power, where stakeholders exercise some share of control over the affairs of an organisation, does not sit easily with a model based on private or public shareholders in which decisions are made not on the basis of one vote for one person in the organisation but on the basis of private ownership of the capital of the organisation or, in the case of a civic organisation, persons appointed by some higher authority and answerable to them mainly or only (such as may be the case in some religious organisations). It is worth mentioning here Wright's definition of democracy (2013, p. 11): 'In a fully democratic society, all people would have broadly equal access to the necessary means to participate meaningfully in decisions about things which affect their lives.'

Fundamental to Wright's definition are (i) all persons and not just some, (ii) equality of access to decisions, and (iii) matters of decision-making that impact on, and matter to, all persons' lives. Inherent to this understanding is the notion of capability used by Amartya Sen (1985). Human capability is the freedom of individuals or groups to live the life they desire or consider as good. Hence, democracy presumes freedom, while freedom is sustained by democratic values and practice.

Wright defines three forms of power: economic, political and social power, all of which are present in any society or organisation. Economic power concerns access to and control over economic resources. Closely allied to economic power is the concept of social power, which concerns the control and influence of voluntary combinations of people in associations of one sort or another (for example, trade unions, churches, cultural movements, political parties, single-issue campaigns or new dispersed online forms of social activism). Political power concerns the exercise of rules, institutions and formal structures of governance and accountability. A transparent, accountable and effective exercise of political power through elections, an independent judiciary, rule of law and accompanied by a free press, freedom of expression and organisation are vital for a functioning democratic society. However, to neglect the concentration of economic or social power would greatly weaken the idea and practice of democracy. Given the nature of production, exchange and distribution in a modern economy, economic power is concentrated in those individuals and corporations with local or worldwide influence, yet also dispersed across the globe and therefore out of the reach of national or even supra-national or inter-governmental agencies such as the United Nations or the European Union.

Peter Katzenstein (1985) argued that European small open economies can reach an accommodation between openness to international market forces and internal social protection. The key to this outcome is a process of negotiation, compromise and adjustment involving different social actors in each case. This type of outcome may be referred to as democratic corporatism. Alternatively, some writers use the term 'Developmental Welfare State' (e.g. Ó Riain, 2014, and the National Economic and Social Council, 2005) to describe a negotiated arrangement modelled on a strong and enabling role for the state in supporting the enterprise economy and social cohesion.

The broad philosophy adopted in the developmental welfare state model advocated by the National Economic and Social Council in 2005 is still relevant (NESC, 2005, p. xix): 'The first public policy challenge is to ensure that every member of Irish society has access to the level and quality of service she or he needs, with quality and equity being assured.'

Taking equality seriously

Closely allied to human rights is the idea of equality – that all persons should be treated with equal respect and accorded equal opportunity and access to participate in society. Equality of access is more important than mere equality of opportunity. Wright (2013, p. 9) makes this clear: 'In a socially just society; all people would have broadly equal access to the social and material conditions necessary for living a flourishing life.'

The unique dignity of each person is respected by a society founded on principles of equality. Some economists approach the concept of equality without due regard for its complex philosophical and ethical dimensions. Equality is more than a statistical measure of inequality in market income or ownership of tangible wealth. Equality concerns respect, affirmation, inclusion and access to power in all the various personal, social, market and state relationships of society. Inequality in income and employment is often allied to that experienced by persons with a disability or because of their gender or ethnicity. Some of the most striking examples of inequality is the systematic disrespect, violence and exclusion experienced by sexual or ethnic groups as well as by a particular section of the population such as children.

Equality, therefore, concerns the capacity, power, freedom and right of individuals or groups to those goods that enable them to realise their well-being. Love, care and solidarity are examples of such goods – goods that cannot be bought, sold or appropriated as forms of economic wealth. Yet, a share of these goods is an important dimension of equality in its widest human sense. We need to acknowledge the idea of equality of access to material and non-material goods and not just equality of opportunity. For example, two students may have equal access to higher education based on their Leaving Certificate results but may not have equality of access to learning resources at home or to costly private grinds because of differences in social class.

Taking sustainability seriously

Wright (2013, p. 12) defines sustainability as follows: 'Future generations should have access to the social and material conditions to live flourishing lives at least at the same level as the present generation.' Everything is connected: poverty, hunger, conflict, migration, environmental degradation and climate change: in other words, the people most vulnerable to the undeniable effects of climate change are those who are already poor and excluded from the major decisions affecting production, trade and investment.

Public discourse about economic and political affairs is dominated by simplistic notions of growth. Growth as quantified in the very restricted definition of GDP provides a very narrow view of total economic well-being. The Canadian economist Osberg

(2001) was instrumental in pioneering the term economic well-being, which has four components: current per capita consumption flows; changes in capital stocks (including natural and human) with an adjustment for an estimated social cost of environmental degradation; changes in income distribution; and changes in economic risks (as measured by economic insecurity from unemployment, ill health, single parent poverty or poverty in old age).

An immediate challenge is whether an improvement in human well-being can be assured while critical dimensions of our social, human and natural environment are under threat.[27] A commitment to investment and growth in GDP is both desirable and unavoidable to enable people to support themselves and to address household and government debt mountains. However, in the long term, pressure on natural resources, including fossil fuels, allied to the clear evidence on rising global temperatures means that an alternative model of development is urgently needed.

Human well-being is conceived as the freedom and capacity to achieve the 'good life' consistent with our values and ideals. As a summary index of such freedom measures of health, education and income are a very proximate indicator of human well-being (as reflected in the thinking and construction of the UN Human Development Index).[28] A vital addition to income, education and health is the freedom to participate in, and contribute to, decision-making in one's society. In other words, equality of opportunity and high levels of education and health do not guarantee democratic choice or freedom if we are denied the freedom to express our views and work with others to bring about change.

Consumption of economic goods and political and civil liberties are secondary to the capacity of exercising choice based on knowledge, health and access to material resources. Hence – following Sen's definition – well-being is defined more by the freedom to achieve according to one's goals than the fact of the achievement itself. Any measure based on income is limited because it tells us nothing about the quality of life, the opportunities open to people and the sustainability of consumption and production.

In addressing the problem of environmental degradation, it is not possible for nation states to achieve the necessary quantum leap on their own – yet inter-governmental gatherings and agreed statements are not sufficient either. There is a once-off opportunity for the European Union to prove that a strong federal or supra-national body based on principles of solidarity and subsidiarity (that is, with delegation of powers to the national level where possible and agreed) can lead the way in tackling global warming. It has the potential political economic and diplomatic power to do so.

3

What Sort of European Dream for Ireland?

What role does the European Union play at global level and how can Ireland be part of this international effort in support of real democracy, full equality and sustainability?

Where we have come from

The EU is considered a huge economic success for the Republic of Ireland and for Northern Ireland. Employment in the Republic doubled in the space of twenty years up to 2007, living standards (especially in the Republic) surged forward and conditions were created for the emergence of a peace process in Northern Ireland.

Membership of the European Union has helped to raise living standards and investment in human capital over the last half century and has also been directly associated with progressive social, environmental and labour market legislation and directives. Before the term Brexit was ever coined, EU membership acted as a de facto stopgap for the 1998 Belfast Agreement as well as a guarantor for the partial development of the all-island economy. Many of the improvements in social and labour market conditions have been associated with membership of the European Union – notwithstanding pre-Brexit opt-outs by the UK in some areas of social and labour market policy.

But there is a darker side to EU membership. Kirby and Murphy (2011, p. 159) described the Irish experience of the EU:

> The burden being imposed on Irish taxpayers to ensure that European banks get repaid for their risky investments at the cost of a lengthy period of severe austerity for Irish citizens shows the extent to which the EU now functions as a mechanism for protecting the economic interests of large companies rather than the social interests of citizens.

Ireland is part of the European continent. To define the membership of the European Union as 'Europe' is to lump together 750 million individuals and a huge mix of cultures, histories and philosophies. No single language, religion or socio-economic model describes Europe, which has been torn apart by war for most of its history and partitioned for half of the last century by a barrier that ran for thousands of kilometres from the Baltic to the Adriatic. Modern Europe is still riven by national rivalries, mistrust and inter-ethnic tension. The rise of populist movements in various EU member states and beyond illustrates a deep-seated malaise and distrust as well as an acute sense of being left behind. Further afield, the dramatic political changes in the US and the threats to world trade as well as the rising challenge of China place a spotlight on Europe.

So what sort of European Union within Europe is desirable and possible for the 450 million citizens within its borders? In the future, along with other parts of the world, the EU component of Europe will face economic slowdowns as well as political, migration-related and environmental crises. To survive, prosper and regrow its membership, it will need a clear vision that appeals to a majority of citizens in each member state. It needs to be built on solid foundations and not merely the shifting sands of short-term political calculus or populist considerations. Above all, to survive and even flourish, the European Union must deliver the three Ps of peace, prosperity and protection for all or most of its citizens. History demonstrates that empires, compacts and alliances that do not deliver on these three Ps do not hold together in the long term. While peace, prosperity and protection are not synonymous with happiness, it is a safe bet that entities that fail to deliver on all three will not deliver on happiness and if most of the people are sufficiently unhappy some of the time or some of the people all the time, the project will not last.

The relatively narrow decision, in June 2016, by the UK to exit the European Union marks a turning point in European history. As the process of UK disengagement from the European Union proceeds, a huge challenge opens up for the EU to remain relevant and to offer a different type of social arrangement to that likely to be on offer in the UK. Brexit has changed everything. This is most evident in the case of Ireland as a whole. British departure from the EU may not be the last such departure. At the same time one cannot exclude the possibility that the UK might re-enter the EU later this century.

An important consideration for all of Ireland is the manner in which the Belfast Agreement of 1998 simply assumed continuing membership of the European Union together with its customs union and single market. All of this underpinned the political agreements of that time and the ensuing process of political reform and partnership. The process of Brexit spells a future of uncertainty and disruption for both parts of the island of Ireland but especially Northern Ireland, which already suffers distinct regional disadvantages within the UK.

The evolution of the European Union

The creation of the European Coal and Steel Community (ECSC) in 1951 on the ashes of a world war that destroyed much of Europe signalled the beginning of a new project of uniting old enemies and creating the conditions for positive cooperation. This project also signalled a cooperation of some Western European countries in political, economic and ideological opposition to communism in the immediate aftermath of 1945.

In time, the ECSC evolved into the EEC, then the European Community and finally the European Union, representing a long-term ambitious political project to create not just a single and free-moving market for goods, services, labour and capital, but a single political compact with a high degree of fiscal, monetary and social policy coordination. Compromises have been made along the way to get to where the project is now. A social dimension including regional and social funding and protection of citizen and labour rights was emphasised in the 1980s as a way of furthering the cohesion of the project and the approval of member states.

The union includes a diverse range of countries, of which fourteen member states were not Western parliamentary democracies in 1970. The move to create a single euro currency in 1999[29] with integration of monetary policies and strict oversight of fiscal policies signalled important shifts in the degree to which any member state can adopt policies or laws at variance with those agreed by international treaty or by the rules and laws of the European Union and its various institutions. The EU is a combination of liberal democracies with varying national-level and EU-pooled social policies and directives between other major world blocks. A sense of shared values and mutual interest binds the union together.

From its inception on the ruins of post-war Western Europe, the European Union project was always anchored on a vision of strong political sovereignty allied to a transition to a single market and set of market rules. But the social dimensions and emphasis of the project have been weakened in the intervening decades. This reflects three mutually reinforcing trends:

- Geopolitical factors with the enlargement of the union to include twelve former communist states, many of which have embraced pronounced forms of neo-liberalism in reaction to their experiences before 1990;
- National political factors, not least the dominant role of a reunited Germany and the influence of ordoliberalist

economic policies implemented in the 1990s and first decade of this century and its adoption into the thinking and rules of the EU and the Eurozone component of the EU;

– Ideological factors with the rise and triumph of neo-liberalism first experimented with in Chile in the 1970s and then powerfully inaugurated in the US under President Reagan and in the UK under Prime Minister Thatcher (and continued under Prime Minister Blair).

Neo-liberalism, as a political idea and project, typically defines policies that limit the role of the state and maximise the freedom of capital over labour. It has dominated the international landscape just as neoclassical economics have dominated thinking and teaching about the economy. Hatched in the laboratory of ideas following World War II, the idea of a small state and a dominant role for markets developed from a marginal movement of thought and political influence to capturing overwhelming support in the US and the UK.

The severe difficulties confronting the post-war settlement in Western Europe as well as the New Deal that predated World War II in the US meant that a new way forward had to be found. Rising oil prices, geopolitical tensions and a deadly combination of price inflation and high unemployment provided a fertile ground for the growth a new kind of politics. In many ways, the Reagan-Thatcher counter-revolution along with the rise of ordo-liberalism in the newly united Germany, which capitalised on various emerging trends, was just as historically significant as the Russian Revolution some sixty years earlier.

Milton Friedman laid out his ideas in the 1982 preface to his signature treatise, *Capitalism and Freedom* (originally published in 1962):

> Only a crisis – actual or perceived – produces real change. When that crisis occurs, the actions that are taken depend on the ideas that are lying around... Our basic function

[is] to develop alternatives to existing policies, to keep them alive and available until the politically impossible becomes the politically inevitable.

This line of thinking leads to a world view that sees radical deregulation, privatisation of national industries and deep cuts to the welfare state as 'politically inevitable'.

Ordoliberalism is a close cousin of neo-liberalism. An early pioneer of ordoliberalism was the German Minister for Finance and Chancellor, Ludwig Erhard.[30] It represents a specifically German application and adaptation of neo-liberalism with a concession in relation to a social market economy and a somewhat stronger role for the state but still bound by tight rules on debt and savings as well as avoidance of significant price inflation. In many respects the European Union reflects the dominance of ordoliberalism in the orientation of its stated fiscal and monetary objectives even though Germany itself fell short of ordoliberalist rules in the years leading up to the recession of 2008–9.

The face of Europe has changed dramatically in recent decades and it would be no exaggeration to say that the four horsemen of the neo-liberal and ordoliberal apocalypse have been in ascendancy in the European body politic:

- Privatisation in the name of competition, efficiency, choice and fiscal prudence.
- The legacy of internal competitive devaluation with downward pressure on wages in some countries deemed to be experiencing a lack of competitiveness and imbalances in trade (McDonnell and O'Farrell, 2015).
- Increased labour market flexibility in the name of global cost competitiveness, foreign direct investment in Europe and efficiencies.
- Incentive-compatible cuts to social welfare to reduce public spending and overcome claimed disincentives to work, frequently aimed at people outside or on the margins of

the workforce such as migrants, lone parents, persons with disabilities and the young.

Just as the UK and the US were moving to the right from about 1980 onwards, the European Union was beginning to adopt the new ideology, interpreting EU rules on competition and open procurement in a manner that favoured the rights of capital over labour. A significant development with regard to labour rights was the rulings by the European Court of Justice on Laval and Viking Line.[31] These rulings in combination with EU policy show how the European legal framework has been evolving – and not necessarily in the interests of workers.

The dominance of fiscal conservatism – especially from 2010 onwards – in response to the financial crisis of 2008–9 placed huge strains on European solidarity. It has also been accompanied by a rise in intergovernmentalism to the detriment of a union of equals. The price of membership in the European club, and, especially in the common currency union, is adherence to what is essentially a neo-liberal agenda. When the people of any member state elect a government that challenges this agenda – as witnessed in 2015 in Greece – there is a possibility of political crisis, which could even threaten the stability of the euro currency itself, not to mention the coherence of the European Union as a whole. Tough negotiation and some degree of compromise and flexibility may buy time but the fundamental contradictions between unbridled market liberalism and bond market hegemony on the one hand and national democracy on the other has not been resolved.

An initially radical left government was elected in Greece in January 2015. Following months of difficult negotiations and unprecedented pressure by the institutions and other governments of the European Union, the ruling left coalition in Greece succumbed to the policy directions from the EU in July 2015. The irony is that democracy died a quick death in Greece in the summer of 2015 – despite the concept having originated there.

Writers such as Wolfgang Streeck (2014) have posited the existence of two mutually conflicting 'states', using the German terms, the *Staatsvolk* and the *Marktvolk*. The *Staatsvolk* describes the citizens' tax state, which is answerable to voters and taxpayers, while the *Marktvolk* is the public debt state answerable to market sentiment and cooperation. According to Streeck, loyalty to the *Staatsvolk* is at odds with the acceptance of the *Marktvolk* during periods of prolonged austerity and diminution in the social well-being of citizens. Whereas the tax state is subject to periodic change or endorsement through elections, the debt state is subject to periodic evaluation through auctions for government bonds. The debt state by its nature and constituencies is embedded fully in international capital markets while the tax state is, still, essentially a national entity. Loyalty of citizens to governments struggling with debt and problems of growth is matched against confidence of markets in the ability of nation states to pay back debt and to grow in the future (the latter being very much tied to the former). Streeck comments (2014, p. 114):

> Since in Europe it is not yet possible, in the name of economic rationality, to do away with the remnants of national democracy especially the accountability of governments to their voters, the method of choice is to integrate national governments into a non-democratic supranational regime – a kind of international superstate without democracy – and have their activities regulated by it.

Can the European Union be reformed?

The EU institutions of monetary policy and fiscal control are not adequate to the task of consolidating economic recovery and social cohesion. A dysfunctional monetary policy ties the hands of the European Central Bank in a way consistent with a price inflation target and without regard for its impact on investment and consumption, both of which are key to economic sustainability. Following the *Five Presidents' Report* (Juncker, 2015) and subsequent statements of intent on the future of EU reform and deepening of the union, the European Commission has set out a roadmap with ambitious targets stretching out to 2025. Included in the Commission proposals are a European Monetary Fund; integration of the Fiscal Compact into EU law; acceleration of structural reforms including those that relate to the labour market at national level; a European Minister of Economy and Finance; and new budgetary instruments for a stable euro area within the Union framework.

In September 2017 Donald Tusk, President of the European Council stated, 'As regards EMU reform, following the publication of the Five Presidents' Report, no one should have any doubts about what we need to do. Everything is crystal clear.' The French President Emmanuel Macron speaks of four imperatives: solidarity and strength in the face of threats from within and without; unity and cooperation in addressing institutional weaknesses; courage in sticking to the plan; and to act with urgency. It is regrettable that part of Macron's plan is to dismantle social protection and the acquis (gains) of post-war progress with regard to labour and social legislation. In 2018 both the German Chancellor Angela Merkel and President Macron strongly endorsed the establishment of an EU army – a proposal that would be of concern to many in Ireland.

The survival of the euro has been called into question by, among others, Joseph Stiglitz (2016), but whether it unravels into two or more currency blocks remains to be seen. What is increasingly clear is that the current single currency regime will not survive without speedy progress to a single banking union, mutualisation of debt (with the creation of Eurobonds), a common deposit insurance mechanism and a set of rules about trade and capital imbalances. Movement in the direction of a fiscal transfer union[32] is required and this is most unlikely to happen in the short to medium term, given current and foreseeable political configurations among the EU states.

The options are stark: further political integration to complete the job begun in the 1980s or a break up in the union or the Eurozone. Neither option is appealing given the political, market and social vulnerability of economically weaker member states. At the same time, muddling through does not appear to be a viable option in the long run. The emergence of new political forces poses a major challenge to a narrow technocratic model of governance in Europe.

The best one can hope for is that the current populist wave washes through while a stronger and reinvigorated centre left regains ground in the key EU states. However, 'social Europe' will need to connect to citizens in a far more concrete manner. We are still far from realising this.

The challenge of Euroscepticism

English nationalism gave us Brexit. But is there a remote possibility of a departure of the Republic of Ireland from membership of the EU, that is, Irexit? The knee-jerk reaction is that 'this could never happen here' or 'Ireland is different', but one must wonder about the depth of commitment to the European project when specific national inter-ests are at stake. How prepared is the Republic of Ireland for further political, fiscal, monetary, social and even military integration when, for many in the upper echelons of our society, Ireland's low headline corporation tax rate of 12.5 per cent should be defended at all costs, and opposition to the Common Corporate Tax Base (CCTB) and a European digital tax is seen as being in the 'national' interest?

The European Commission has recently challenged Ireland on competition grounds in relation to the special treatment of particular large multinationals for the purposes of corporation tax. Here we have the ironic spectacle of a country that had been deeply traumatised by the social impacts of austerity appealing a €13 billion tax settlement. The European Commission says Ireland should have collected this money and used it to pay for key public services and infrastructural investment. In this instance, it seems the European Commission is much too kind to Ireland!

A significant driver of right-wing Euroscepticism is insecurity about perceived threats arising from immigration. Opposition to migration and freedom of movement as well as the intake of refugees (still a major issue for member states in south-east Europe) has helped stoke opposition movements that threaten to pull apart the EU. The success or otherwise of these movements will depend on how the EU can deliver on peace, prosperity and protection for its citizens. It is notable that in Ireland, even today, explicit and visible expressions of racism or mistrust towards immigrants are confined and limited in a way that is the envy of other countries. However, this could change rapidly.

One detects an amplification in soft Euroscepticism from certain quarters of the Irish media and commentariat, currently focusing on national sovereignty and the alleged evils of Brussels-imposed norms on corporate taxation. It also finds expression in the liberal doctrine that Ireland belongs to the Anglo-American world along with its rediscovered ideology of small states and 'free' enterprises – that is freed from social constraints and checks and balances. The intrusion of an aggressive type of home-grown nationalism from Britain may very well find echoes on this island, not so much over immigration (although the ugly head of racism is raised) but over the identification of the EU with all things bad and the false promise of the new dawn of a new small state. Many social commentators and political interests have greatly underestimated, in a wider global context, the power, attraction and influence of nationalism and even religion – which is sometimes conflated with nationalism as well as post-colonial cultural and social identities. Such identities and loyalties do matter, even in a post-modern society.

Has the Nordic Model a future?

Capitalism comes in many varieties, some of which coexist within the structures of the European Union (Hall and Soskice, 2001). Yet a potent mixture of internal political pressure, the continuing external pressure of globalisation, and neo-liberalism is blurring the edges between the variants.

The term 'Nordic Model' describes a set of economic, social and political arrangements loosely common to all five Scandinavian countries: Denmark, Finland, Iceland, Norway and Sweden. These arrangements include a broad element of pragmatism, consensus and cooperation in relation to a social market economy as well as high levels of productivity and market flexibility combined with low levels of social and economic inequality. The state has a strong role – as do civil society organisations – in providing a framework for development. Relatively high taxes pay for social goods and services such as childcare, education, health and other areas. At the same time these countries remain very much integrated into global and national systems of privately owned and, on the whole, well-regulated enterprises. There is a greater freedom to fail initially without being a societal failure.

Of course, there is no single Nordic Model, as each Scandinavian country has adopted a different approach to a given area of social policy. Moreover, the model has undergone significant change and modification in recent decades and is increasingly under strain due to the global pressure to reduce business costs, shrink the size of the public sphere and liberalise the use and movement of capital and labour across national boundaries. Businesses in Scandinavia are subject to intense competition on all fronts, making it a challenge to maintain high levels of tax and welfare provision. Some analysts interpret these recent changes as adaptation to better reflect new conditions and needs, while others take a less benign view (Wahl, 2011), seeing it as a global trend towards a smaller state and the privatisation of public goods and services.

Begg (2016) proposes that Ireland can still build on what has been achieved. He argues that Ireland needs a Rehn-Meidner-type model along the lines of the one constructed by Swedish trade union economists in the 1950s, which shaped today's Nordic Model. This model was developed by two Swedish economists, Gosta Rehn and Rudolf Meidner, working for the Swedish Confederation of Trade

Unions in the early 1950s. Erixon (2008) describes some of the main principles or aims of the model:

- a restrictive fiscal policy combined with restrictive monetary policy to increase public saving and control inflation;
- active labour market policy (ALMP) encompassing retraining and mobility to upskill and ensure engagement in the labour market;
- selective demand-stimulating policy when there is a shortfall in aggregate demand;
- a coordinated wages policy based on the principles of solidarity and equality of pay for equal jobs;
- a central job evaluation to determine fair wage differentials.

The context for the post-war Rehn-Meidner Model was set in Sweden in the years immediately following World War II. This period was characterised by a movement towards full employment in Sweden through expansionary fiscal and monetary policies, the implementation of an incomes policy (entailing price controls and collective wage restraint), exchange rate flexibility including devaluation of the Swedish Kroner and selective fiscal policy measures to combat inflation.

The aim of the emerging political movement was not to replace capitalism with socialism but rather to make capitalism work better in Sweden in a way that promoted economic growth with the benefits more evenly distributed while maintaining social cohesion, industrial peace, price stability and full employment, aside from frictional or temporary periods of unemployment in between jobs and training. In light of developments since the 1950s these points hardly appear radical or disruptive. Even though the model has been adapted, revised and in some respects scaled back, it remains an important benchmark. To the extent that it was applied in Sweden in the 1950s up to the first oil crisis in 1973, it was broadly successful in helping to ensure economic growth, greater social equality as well as fiscal, monetary and price stability. Wage inequality remained low and the scale and quality of public services as well as lifelong learning provision was maintained, as evidenced by recent OECD surveys of skills in the adult population. It does appear that countries with higher levels of economic equality combined with democracy show high levels of human well-being and happiness and lower levels of social dysfunction.

Some remnants of the Rehn-Meidner Model still apply in the use of flexicurity in Denmark. Flexicurity combines flexibility in the labour market (employment in a different enterprise or sector following the loss of a job), social security pegged to income and an active labour market policy with obligations and rights for the unemployed. In order to work, such an arrangement requires adequate taxation (sometimes through systems of social insurance but also through general taxation), high levels of protection of income and employment, sufficient training opportunities and a high degree of social cooperation and buy-in by the key actors.

As Erixon has noted, many aspects of the Rehn-Meidner Model have been modified and even abandoned in Sweden during the 1980s and 1990s yet, along with other Scandinavian countries, it remains a high-productivity, high-wage society. The Nordic Model is under increasing pressure from globalisation, mobility of capital and the political shifts within Europe. The gradual dismantling of capital controls within and outside the European Union since the 1970s has changed the rules of the game for national political economy. The scope for a type of benign social democratic settlement behind national boundaries has become very limited in the absence of a more social Europe.

Three powerful forces combine to make it extremely difficult, if not impossible, to build a type of Nordic Model behind national boundaries:

– The all-pervasive and popular based ideology that asserts the inevitability of globalisation and the prominence of markets over social control.

- The absence of capital controls at national level, exposing sovereign governments to flights of capital or rapid outflows of direct investment in response to shifts in taxes, costs or profits.
- The rules of international competition and outsourcing of commercial services in the public domain, which makes it increasingly difficult for national governments in the EU to pursue public ownership as a policy.

The onset of recession and austerity policies across the EU and the developing crisis in the social democratic political family has opened up a political vacuum, the filling of which poses many questions. With the demise of the large-scale communist parties in France, Italy and other countries as well as the collapse of the Soviet Union and associated countries in 1989–91 there is no longer a strong political force capable of resisting the advance of an aggressive neo-liberalism – especially within the European Union. In most countries trade unions, for a variety of reasons, have been weakened through falling numbers as well as political influence to counteract the worst excesses of economic liberalism.

Given the direction of political movement in Europe in the last two decades it is questionable that the Nordic Model will survive the negative influences of globalisation as well as a European Union increasingly wedded to policies hostile to it. This is reinforced by the strong impetus towards 'more Europe' in the speeches of some key European political leaders in the EU27 (the European Union minus the UK). That said, counter-balancing forces at work in many jurisdictions (the US, the UK and other states including Portugal at the time of writing) indicate a possibility that civil society can be influenced to support a move forward to a new type of capitalism similar to the Nordic Model.

Envisioning a new Europe

Will the European Union evolve into a union of competition and free movement of goods, services, labour and capital without a strong social component? Alternatively, will the Union become one of solidarity and comprehensive human freedoms to which competition and freedom of movement are subordinate? The answer to these questions will, very likely, seal the fate of the EU in the coming decades.

To survive and to flourish the European Union will need to undergo fundamental change. It may be necessary to scale back and even reverse some of the centralising forces pointing in the direction of a unitary or federal superstate, although this is unlikely to happen without the majority support of citizens in all member states. That Europe (and not just the EU) has managed to function without war – with some notable regional excep-tions[33] – should not give grounds for complacency. The drums of national rivalry and mutual suspicion, exacerbated by historical grudges and an appetite for control of key natural resources, spell threats for the future. Only a European accord covering all the main nations of Europe, including Russia, can provide for con-tinuing peace. However, the European Union needs to decide which direction it will take. Perhaps a citizen-led movement in some key member states could help move the entire union back from its centralising and regressive social stance and restore bal-ance by way of social controls on capital and democratic control of public policy.

A big weakness in the institutional architecture of the European Union is the lack of a coherent and internally coordi-nated fiscal, monetary and political union. Elements of each are present but lopsided. Without, for example, a coherent back-up to deal with a large-scale banking crisis, national governments are left with the likelihood of dysfunctional banks straddled with non-performing loans. The size and scale of a backstop at EU level (in the form of the European Stability Mechanism) is insufficient to deal with a large-scale crisis. Moreover, the absence of an effective pooling of at least some parts of sover-eign debt coupled with a cross-border insurance of large-scale banking deposits means that the EU is highly vulnerable to the inevitable future financial shocks. Were the EU to evolve into a United States of Europe (USE) with a significant federal budget accounting for 10 or 20 per cent of collective USE GDP and a single banking system, then it might be in a position to withstand once-in-a-generation shocks. However, this is politically unrealistic for many decades into the future.

It might be possible to put in place an effective system of fiscal transfer as presently holds in countries such as Italy, Spain, Germany and the UK (benefiting Wales, Scotland and Northern Ireland as well as the northern regions of England in the latter), but a fiscal transfer arrangement would presuppose almost universal buy-in from the governments of all EU member states. It could only work on the premises of a type of collective solidarity founded on identity, values and culture. In the case of the US, a common language has been a major bonding factor in the course of evolution from a scattering of colonies in the eighteenth century to a single federation of states. That said, given the tragic history of Europe and the efforts by generations of European citizens and politicians, the prospects of further cooperation and integration of at least some parts of the European Union should not be dismissed as unlikely or impossible.

Although the prospects for reforming and staying in the EU look set for a member state such as the Republic of Ireland, this does not deter citizens from reclaiming the debate about the EU – and this must start from an honest appraisal of where the European Union currently stands. Reform of the Common Agricultural Policy (CAP), which accounts for well over 50 per cent of the total EU budget (itself relatively small compared to the combined GDP of the EU27), could be linked to a new programme of investment in renewable energy and forestry. There is plenty of scope for a long-term switch from methane-emitting animals in Ireland to growing more forests: we have yet to recover from the deforestation programme of the seventeenth century.

A potentially useful way of rebuilding trust and genuine European solidarity would be a cast-iron guarantee that member states in the single euro currency cannot be threatened with a withdrawal of liquidity or expelled from the euro area, as happened with Greece in 2015.

The Marshall Plan of the 1940s (a programme to rebuild Europe from the ravages of war) helped generate growth and transformed entire societies. Likewise, in today's Europe there is a need for vision and generosity in reclaiming lost ground due to recession and the advances of neo-liberalism. A proposal by the German trade union confederation (DGB) in 2013 provided a detailed analysis of how a new programme of investment (also named the Marshall Plan) could help transform the European economy. The annual cost might be in the region of 2 per cent of total EU GDP per annum and could create 10 million additional jobs in Europe as well as save public spending through lower social spending as a result of unemployment or under-employment. A combination of revenue streams were identified, including a community financial transaction tax (FTT). Ireland and other member states should pursue the idea of a coordinated cross-member state FTT. Furthermore, a reversal of Irish policy would send a strong signal to the world that Ireland is ready to do business on tax reform for global justice.

One way to make the EU more relevant to citizens is to develop a European social insurance fund financed by a levy of 1 per cent on each member state and out of which particular additional benefits are payable over a fixed period to people who lose their jobs or take time out of the labour force to engage in training. Another way of making the EU more socially helpful is to establish a European Climate Fund based on a community carbon tax amounting to 1 per cent of GDP applied across all member states: this fund could be invested in renewable energy and interconnectors to peripheral states.

The European Union must be radically reformed to make it more relevant to the needs of most European citizens and this needs to happen within the next generation. Reform can only come about if the balance is restored in such a way that social needs takes primacy over market forces and arbitrary state rules, whether in the domain of national fiscal discretion or various areas of social life. The EU may survive, but only as a smaller, more compact and more socially integrated union. Will Ireland be part of such a union in twenty or thirty years' time? That choice depends on us.

4

Three Big Challenges: Demographic, Technological and Environmental Change

Heraclitus declared that the only constant is change: Ireland and Europe, in the first half of the twenty-first century, bear out this view. Rapid advances in technology and unstable politics, frontiers, institutions and values are the order of the day. Yet millions of people continue to live in poverty. Precariousness and inequality are on the rise.

'But the world is made up of classes, religions and nations' wrote Paul Mason in *Postcapitalism* (2015).[34] Analysts and policymakers ignore the interaction of these three forces at their peril. Fixing the economy and enabling a political peace in today's world is much more than fine-tuning monetary, fiscal or political institutional arrangements. Conflicts of material interest, ideas and loyalties greatly complicate the task on hand. Moreover, the unpredictable will happen, and the predictable will often fail to materialise because of factors that go beyond an explanatory model based on evidence and assumptions from the past. Acknowledging and naming the complex role of social class, religion and nations is therefore important.

The focus of this book – and this chapter in particular – is not on the role of religion or nations but on three big challenges (or opportunities depending on how we see it) that continue to transform societies across the globe: demographic, technological and environmental change. They impact on public finances, the financial system and the readiness of enterprises in both Irish jurisdictions to adapt efficiently.

Add to these three big challenges the fragility and combustible nature of regional and world politics – not to mention the drawn-out drama of Brexit – and the future looks very uncertain. These challenges constitute what might be termed the 'known unknowns'.[35] And then there are the unknown unknowns. To give an example of an unknown unknown, please refer to world history over the last five decades: those things most feared and anticipated (like nuclear war) did not happen, while those things never imagined did. The almost entirely peaceful collapse of communist dictatorships in Eastern Europe and the astonishing boom in world trade and output in the two decades leading up to the recession of 2008–09 bear this out.

A positive part of the demographic landscape of the Republic of Ireland and Northern Ireland is the role of migration in creating a diverse population and workforce. This pattern, which has intensified in recent decades, has created its own challenges and opportunities. As a result of immigration Ireland is a more culturally enriched and interesting place for people in which to live and work. At the same time the ugly spectre of racism is never far from wherever jobs, houses and other social goods are seen as scarce and open to competition. Ireland has known many waves of immigration, from the Celts to the Vikings to the Normans and the Ulster Scots not to mention very significant numbers arriving from various European and non-European countries in recent decades. Diversity is good and moreover, as a relatively wealthy island, we have a responsibility to share some of our prosperity and goods with those who seek refuge for economic or other reasons. After all, millions of Irish emigrants sought a new life during times of famine, oppression and economic under-development including in the recent past, when large numbers of people left the Republic of Ireland during recessions in the 1950s, 1980s and 2009–12.

Inward migration is economically, socially and spiritually positive, but it needs careful management. Among other things, immigrants should have access to rights, public services and opportunities[36] and should adhere to the laws and norms of the host country. A policy of integration is essential with regard to education, housing, employment and other spheres. Thankfully, xenophobia, racism and far-right populism have been relatively limited in the Republic of Ireland and unlike in most other European countries, there has been no far-right or neo-Nazi movement threatening to claim a foothold in electoral terms. However, the threats posed by racism and far-right politics should not be dismissed, even in Ireland. We should be mindful of the deeply embedded prejudice against the Traveller community that can be found in the Republic of Ireland (MacGréil, 2010). In Northern Ireland, the reality of sectarianism and the threat of a resumption of civil conflict is a stark warning.

Demographic change in the Republic of Ireland

Net outward migration has provided a safety release for high levels of unemployment during periods of crisis in Ireland. Over time the nature and composition of regional outward migration has shifted towards relatively high-skilled graduates with a significant inward flow of sometimes highly qualified migrants in response to areas of specific demand. In all likelihood Brexit will add to inward migration to the Republic of Ireland not just by British nationals but by persons and families who might have otherwise migrated to the UK.

The total size of population resident in the Republic of Ireland has risen rapidly since the early 1990s, reflecting a combination of fertility, mortality and migration changes. The rate of growth slowed considerably in the aftermath of the recession of 2008–12, reflecting the resumption of net outward migration

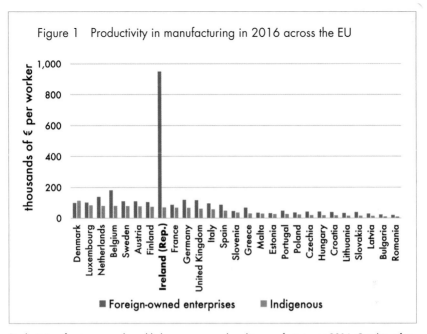

Figure 1   Productivity in manufacturing in 2016 across the EU

Productivity refers to gross value added per person employed in manufacturing in 2016. Czechia refers to the country formerly known as the Czech Republic. Source: Eurostat databank, code [fats_g1a_08].

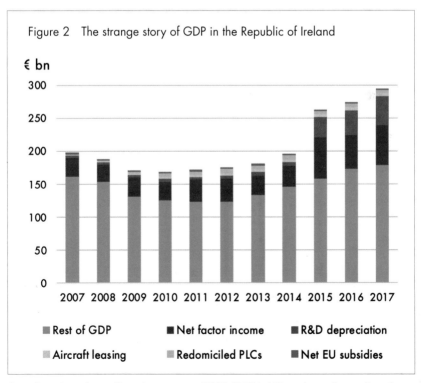

Figure 2   The strange story of GDP in the Republic of Ireland

Gross domestic product and its main components (2007–2017) in billions of euro. Source: Central Statistics Office National Accounts (Annex 1), code [N1724].

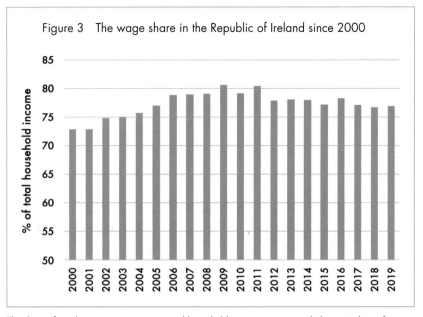

Figure 3 The wage share in the Republic of Ireland since 2000

The share of employee compensation in total household primary income excluding social transfers and before deduction of taxes on income. Source: Central Statistics Office County Accounts, code [CIA01]. Data for 2016–2019 have been estimated by the author based on latest available projections from the ESRI.

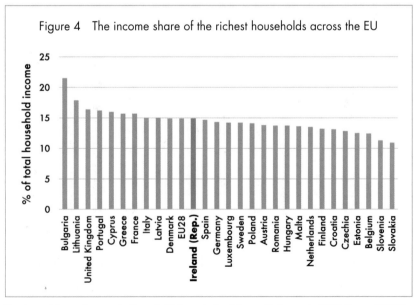

Figure 4 The income share of the richest households across the EU

The share of the top 5 per cent of households in equivalised disposable income in 2017. Source: EU-SILC survey, code [ilc_di01].

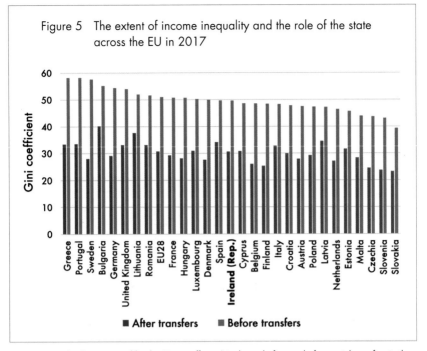

Figure 5 The extent of income inequality and the role of the state across the EU in 2017

Income inequality (as measured by the Gini coefficient) is shown before and after social transfers in the EU28. Data are ranked by the value of the coefficient before transfers. Transfers include state pensions. The Gini coefficient measures inequality. Its value approaches 100 when a society is perfectly unequal and approaches 0 when perfectly equal. The higher the value the greater the degree of inequality. Source: Eurostat databank EUSILC, codes [ilc_di12 and ilc_di12b].

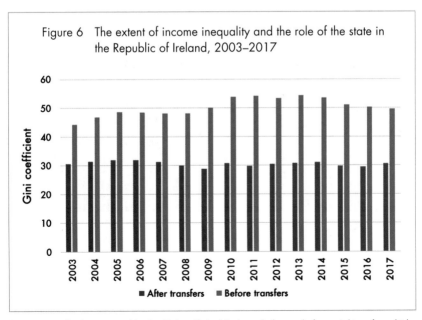

Figure 6 The extent of income inequality and the role of the state in the Republic of Ireland, 2003–2017

Income inequality (as measured by the Gini coefficient) is shown before and after social transfers which include state pensions. Source: Eurostat databank EUSILC, codes [ilc_di12 and ilc_di12b].

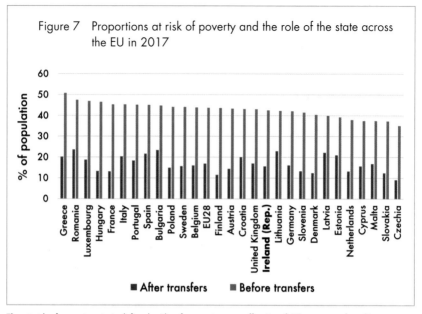

Figure 7   Proportions at risk of poverty and the role of the state across the EU in 2017

The at risk of poverty rate is defined with reference to a cut-off point of 60 per cent of median equivalised income before and after social transfers in 2017. Source: Eurostat databank EUSILC, codes [ilc_li09b & ilc_li03].

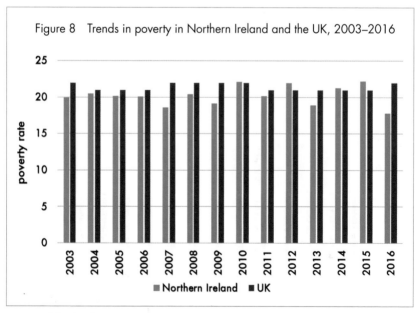

Figure 8   Trends in poverty in Northern Ireland and the UK, 2003–2016

Poverty is defined as the percentage of the population with an income below 60 per cent of the UK median. Income is adjusted for inflation and household size and is after housing costs are taken into account. Source: Family Resources Survey (Department for Communities).

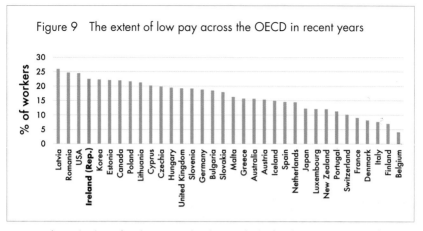

Figure 9   The extent of low pay across the OECD in recent years

Low pay refers to the share of workers earning less than two-thirds of median earnings. Data refer to full-time employees. Data for the following countries refer to 2017: Canada, Czechia, Japan, Korea, Slovakia and the US. Data for the following countries refer to 2015: Iceland and Lithuania. Data for the following countries refer to 2014: Bulgaria, Cyprus, Estonia, France, Latvia, Luxembourg, Malta, Netherlands, Romania, Slovenia and Spain. Data for all other countries, including the Republic of Ireland, refer to 2016. Source: OECD (2019), wage levels (indicator) doi: 10.1787/0a1c27bc-en.

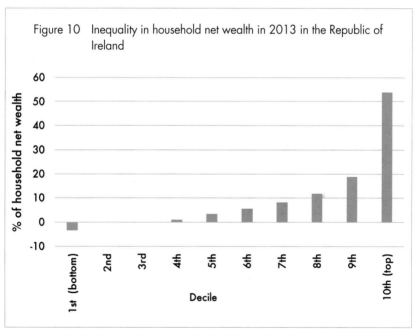

Figure 10   Inequality in household net wealth in 2013 in the Republic of Ireland

Percentage distribution of net wealth for households. In 2013, the richest 10 per cent of households owned 54 per cent of total household net wealth. Source: Lawless and Lynch (2016).

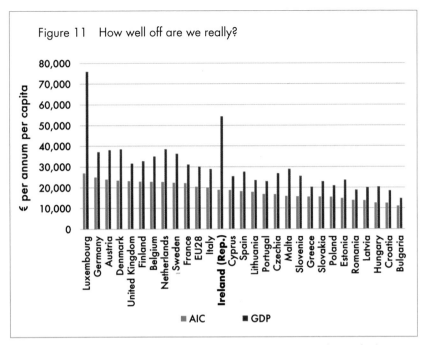

Figure 11   How well off are we really?

Data refer to 2017. Actual individual consumption (AIC) in € per capita is a rough proxy for 'living standards'. It includes the value of public services. Source: Eurostat databank, code [prc_ppp_ind].

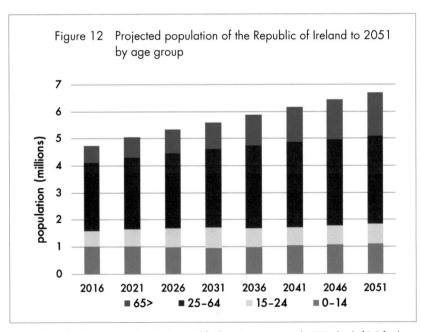

Figure 12   Projected population of the Republic of Ireland to 2051 by age group

Data are based on CSO assumption, F1, i.e., total fertility rate to remain at the 2016 level of 1.8 for the lifetime of the projections, and M1, i.e., assumed net inward migration of 30,000 per annum from 2018 onwards. Source: Central Statistics Office, current population and labour force projections, code [PEA22].

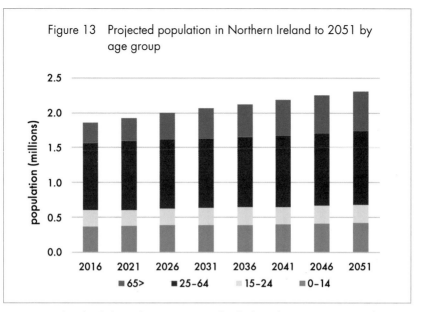

Figure 13 Projected population in Northern Ireland to 2051 by age group

Projections are based on high-growth assumptions regarding fertility and migration. Source: Northern Ireland Statistics and Research Agency.

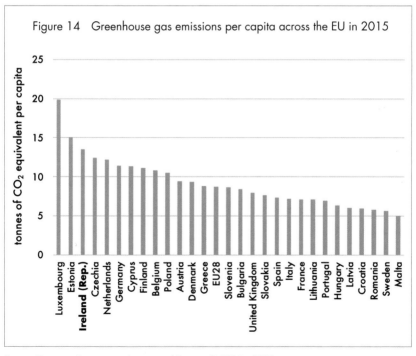

Figure 14 Greenhouse gas emissions per capita across the EU in 2015

Source: European Environment Agency and Eurostat [Rt2020_rd300].

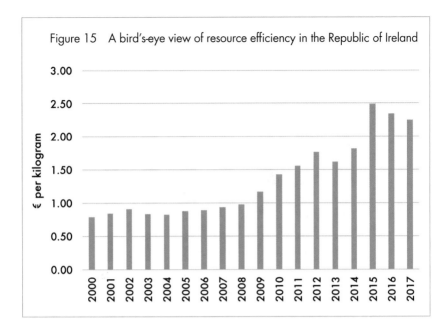

Figure 15   A bird's-eye view of resource efficiency in the Republic of Ireland

Figure 15 & Figure 16: euro values are adjusted for price differences, i.e., purchasing power standard (PPS) values. Efficiency is measured by the ratio of GDP to domestic material consumption (euros per kilogram at constant purchasing power standard). Source: Eurostat, material flow accounts [env_ac_rp].

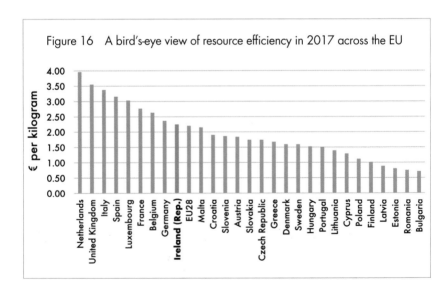

Figure 16   A bird's-eye view of resource efficiency in 2017 across the EU

– albeit at a lower rate as measured relative to 1,000 of population – compared to the 1980s or 1950s when large-scale net outward migration occurred. The total number of births remains at a high level – the highest since the late nineteenth century even though the fertility rate has fallen and was at a level of 1.8 in 2017 (the replacement rate is 2.1). A changing population structure with a larger number of women in the 25–40 age bracket coupled with a very modest recovery in the fertility rate since the 1990s pushed births up to an annual rate of over 75,000 up to 2010. Since then, the annual total of live births has fallen back to 62,000 in 2017.

The latest population and labour force projections issued by the CSO (2018b) reflect various assumptions and scenarios considered, at the time of publication, in the light of census data published in 2016. It should be noted that the actual population recorded in 2016 exceeded all of the six possible scenarios posited in the CSO projections report issued in 2013. The highest projected population for 2016 was 4,704,100 persons while the actual population recorded was 4,761,865.

Projected population depends on assumptions regarding births, deaths[37] and migration. These show a range from 5.2 million to 5.6 million persons in 2031 and a range of 5.6 million to 6.7 million in the year 2051. The population age structure will change depending on what patterns of migration, mortality and fertility prevail.

The projection of a larger and older population has implications for social spending and public services. Assuming constant or even declining labour force participation rates, it is estimated that 'age-related' public expenditure[38] will increase from a projected figure of 29.4 per cent of GDP in 2015 to 33.6 per cent in 2060.[39] However, age-related public spending is not expected to increase significantly between 2015 and 2030 (Connors, Duffy and Newman, 2016).

It could be claimed that the Republic of Ireland and Northern Ireland have a demographic advantage over many other European regions in so far as they have experienced a late fall in the number of births followed by a stabilisation in the numbers during the last two decades. A demographic 'slow start' of approximately 15 to 20 years compared to most other European countries means that the full pressure of ageing societies will not be felt, here, until about the middle of this century. This is in spite of a growth in the number and proportion of persons aged 65 and over in the immediate years ahead. The impact of there being more over-65s in the population is offset against a rise in the size of the 'working-age' population (aged 15–64). Figure 12 shows a scenario based on fast growth in total population from 4.8 million in 2016 to 6.7 million in 2051 in the Republic of Ireland. Under this scenario, the 'working-age dependency ratio' falls, gradually, from 1.1 to 0.9. This measure is defined as the ratio of projected population, aged 25–64, to the combined total of persons aged 0–14 or 65 and over. However, the proportion of the population aged 65 years or older rises sharply from 13.6 per cent of total population in 2016 to 16.3 per cent in 2026; and to 23.9 per cent in 2051.

Were population to grow at a much slower rate, the proportion of 65-year-olds and over would rise to 27.4 per cent by 2051. These orders of projected increases will place new and additional pressures on public and private costs of pensions, health, long-term care and suitable accommodation for senior citizens.[40]

As in any projections exercise, there is considerable uncertainty in actual outcomes as patterns of migration and fertility are difficult to foresee and are related to many other factors. It is highly likely that in the event of continuing strong economic performance in the Republic of Ireland and the avoidance of another 'lost decade' in a future economic shock, that a pattern of strong inward migration will continue to be a feature of Irish demographics. An increase in inward migration will ease, somewhat, the pressure of an ageing population. However, the health, pension and other costs associated with ageing will be considerable no matter what demographic scenario is assumed. In the case of inward migration additional demand for housing and other public services will arise. At the same time, given the age and skills profile of immigrants to Ireland, productivity and government revenue will be higher than otherwise would have been the case.

Demographic change in Northern Ireland

Compared to the Republic of Ireland the total size of population resident in Northern Ireland has risen more slowly since the early 1990s. This reflects a different combination of fertility, mortality and migration changes. The latest population and labour force projections issued by the Northern Ireland Statistical and Research Agency (NISRA, 2018a) indicate a number of possible scenarios and population outcomes up to the year 2051 and beyond. In Figure 13, a relatively fast growth in population is projected based on a set of assumptions: a gradual increase in the fertility rate from 1.9 in 2016 to replacement level of 2.1 in the mid-2030s; and a small increase in net inward migration to Northern Ireland. This yields a growth in total population from an estimated 1.86 million in 2016 to 2.31 million by 2051.

Combining population projections for both jurisdictions, it is possible that total population for the island of Ireland could reach 9 million by the middle of the century, thus exceeding the peak in population on the island in 1841. Were inward migration – a highly unstable and difficult to predict variable – significantly higher than assumed either by the CSO or NISRA, population might very well exceed 10 million by the middle of the century. This compares to an estimated combined total of 6.8 million on the island of Ireland in 2019. This scale of possible or likely population growth will place huge demands on our healthcare systems, education, childcare, public transport, housing and other areas of public services and collective social goods.

Population growth will also increase the store of human skill and diversity with economic and social benefits. It is noticeable that the rate of population is likely to be significantly higher in the Republic of Ireland than in Northern Ireland. The key difference seems to lie in patterns of inward migration.

Technological change, automation and the future of work

Forty years ago when I joined the staff of the ESRI in Dublin as a research assistant I carried out my number-crunching with a large physical sheet of paper, a cumbersome gadget called a calculator and, with Tippex and thinner solution to hand, I wrote up the results and submitted them to the typing pool consisting of a large number of trained typists. Analysis of large datasets involved trips to a special computer centre where hundreds of punch cards containing esoteric computer language codes held together with a rubber band were left in for an overnight run (the following morning a folding sheet print-out would spit out 'job aborted' and you started all over again!). Journeys to a library were an essential part of the job. Today, I access economic journal articles on something online while using open source software to locate, number-crunch and draft up. Where tomes of annual statistical reports lay on shelves it is now possible to electronically bookmark links to online databases containing thousands of tables and 10,000s of information items available from Eurostat, the CSO or NISRA.

If our work has changed so much in the last forty years, what will the next thirty bring? For sure, rapid changes in technology will continue to transform the way we live and the manner in which businesses trade and communicate (Kinsella, 2009). New and faster connections facilitate a rapid exchange of information as well as a consolidation of huge stores of data that transcend national boundaries and regulations. Real-time technology has transformed the way public and private services are delivered. These changes have reinforced globalisation and trade and have impacted on the structure of demand for skills and knowledge. Many back-office jobs can be relocated to distant locations on the globe, while the crucial role of digital literacy and capacity in almost all walks of life and commerce is greatly enhanced. Systems of education, public administration, security and business are scarcely able to keep pace with the speed and depth of change.

Anyone in the mid-1980s considering the future evolution of technology would never have guessed the extent, scale and nature of innovation that has occurred where little computers lie in our pocket and we can watch television, chat with someone on the other side of the world through FaceTime or other applications and where we can conduct our banking business by means of a few clicks. Yet significant digital divides exist within advanced economies and post-industrial societies with particular groups less likely to access new technology for reasons of finance, training or habit. Add to this the regional broadband divide whereby households and businesses still cannot effectively use the Internet in many rural parts of Ireland. New digital technologies, although spreading rapidly, have yet to reach billions of citizens in poorer regions of the globe.

The revolution in technology is not confined to the digital world. Huge changes in manufacturing, outsourcing, off-shoring and the rise of borderless companies transferring activities across frontiers and booking their profits and tax bills in different locations have greatly complicated the nature of production and political control. Globalisation in trade, finance and knowledge has had mixed effects. In some cases, it has transformed for the better living standards and conditions of education and health for large populations. In other cases, it has triggered rising inequalities, displacement of workers, impoverishment of particular regions and countries as well as causing long-term environmental damage. Every perceived benefit comes with an economic, social and environmental price. Changes in the organisation of production and relocation of activity have undermined, in many cases, employment rights and standards with a rise in precarious, outsourced and involuntary self-employed work patterns. While these changes have been acclaimed as enhancing freedom of movement and competition, they have also spread insecurity and have triggered a breakdown in social solidarity where new workers frequently experience inferior conditions, sick pay, maternity leave and pensions rights compared to previous generations.

The future of work in specific sectors and occupations in particular is of concern. Frey and Osborne (2017) estimated that 47 per cent of US employment is at risk in some way due to artificial intelligence (AI). This is also likely to be a feature of most European labour markets, including Ireland. Clerical, administrative, service and retail jobs are particularly vulnerable, as witnessed by the outsourcing of payroll and HR functions in large organisations to shop workers displaced by self-service checkouts to online banking services instead of high street branches.

Recent research for the OECD (Nedelkoska and Quintini, 2018) placed Ireland halfway among OECD countries in terms of exposure to job loss or significant change in job tasks as a result of automation. Across the OECD world, it is estimated that 1 in 7 jobs are at high risk from AI while a further 1 in 3 are likely to undergo significant change as a result. However, many jobs, such as teaching, personal health care and childcare, are heavily reliant on interpersonal, emotional communication as well as individual and collective creativity – skills that do not lend themselves to automation processes. The more routine and predictable a task or set of operations are, the easier it is to introduce forms of AI.

Using estimates contained in OECD publications, some 350,000 jobs in the Republic of Ireland are at high risk of displacement while a further 600,000 could be significantly changed as a result of AI. Corresponding figures for Northern Ireland are difficult to estimate but based on UK trends, some 100,000 jobs could be at risk with a further 200,000 subject to significant change. Research by Foster and Wilson (2019) using the task-based approach to estimating the impact of AI suggests a figure of around 57,000 jobs at high risk in Northern Ireland. The manufacturing and agriculture sectors are most impacted by these changes, although some areas of services, including public administration and healthcare, are also affected. Young people, in particular, could be more vulnerable to the extent that entrant positions even for highly educated young persons are disproportionately automatable (examples of which could arise in areas such as accountancy and the legal profession).

Have we reached a new stage of capitalism in which the nature of work, social class relations and commerce has changed? Mason (2015) refers to a new order called 'postcapitalism' in which new forms of social knowledge produced under conditions of shared knowledge and 'free' information goods – a by-product of new technology – are radically changing the rules, including our notions of scarcity, market power and even work itself. There is some truth in these claims but the extent of transformation may be exaggerated. The concentration of financial and political power in the hands of elites and the dependence of most people on labour to provide a living has not gone away. Human work still remains at the heart of social progress and the question of ownership of the means of production still challenges us to think out new and diverse forms of enterprise and social organisation.

The local impact of the global environmental challenge

There are no jobs on a dead planet. And the lives of the next generation will be affected dramatically by climate change. Estimated anthropogenic global warming is estimated to be increasing at around 0.2°C per decade as a result of past and current emissions. In its 2018 report, the Intergovernmental Panel on Climate Change (IPCC) revised previous policy objectives, focusing on a limitation of average global temperature increases from 2° by the end of this century to 1.5° by 2030. This, it argues, is the minimum needed to avoid catastrophic impact, some of which is already all too evident in terms of extreme weather events and large shifts in ice coverage within the Arctic and Antarctic Circles.

The combination of climate change, energy supply and energy cost provide a huge challenge to societies across the globe. For Ireland, the challenge is twofold: anticipating and preparing for likely or possible adverse changes in energy supply and cost in the futures including unforeseen or sudden disruptions to supply of imported fossil fuel energy; and modifying human behaviour and public policy as part of a global and local ethic to protect the planet and leave a better world for future generations.

Changes in attitude, behaviour and public policy is a long-term, complex, and urgent project. Climate change constitutes the greatest single challenge and opportunity for societies in the twenty-first century, which needs to be reflected in political economy and in public policy across the globe. Waiting for international agreement is not an option. An overriding priority must be to significantly reduce greenhouse gas emissions over the coming decades and hasten an energy transition beyond fossil fuels. New targets need to be set for the next half century and policies must be regularly monitored and evaluated.

The weight of scientific evidence strongly indicates that a long-term and profound shift has occurred in global temperatures and this is likely to be related, among other possible factors, to an acceleration in the burning of fossil fuels since the onset of the industrial revolution in the eighteenth century. The decade ending 2010 was the hottest on record; the one ending 2020 is almost certain to exceed it.

The European Commission has stated that:

CO_2 is the greenhouse gas most commonly produced by human activities and it is responsible for 64 per cent of man-made global warming ... the current global average temperature is 0.85°C higher than it was in the late nineteenth century. Each of the past three decades has been warmer than any preceding decade since records began in 1850.[41]

In the Republic of Ireland, fossil fuels account for only 70 per cent of total CO_2 emissions, with the remainder coming from deforestation, industrial agriculture and associated soil degradation and release of methane gas by livestock (which is particularly damaging in its impact), cement production and landfill effects.

Switching to clean energy is only part of a policy response to climate change.

The way energy is used will assume even greater importance as the cumulative effects of soil degradation and deforestation become more apparent. A growth-driven planet with a stipulation of 3 per cent annual growth means a doubling of production every twenty years and, in the absence of significant production and consumption changes, would involve twice as much extraction and degradation every twenty years thereafter. While technological innovations are required to decouple production and consumption from carbon-based energy sources the debate about human development needs to be reframed as being much more about quality and distribution than an ever-ending drive to increase output of commodities (Barry, 2018).

Ireland's pattern of fast growth in the decade up to 2007 was characterised by a relatively high carbon content. At 2.88 tonnes of CO_2 equivalent per capita, the Republic of Ireland was the highest of any EU28 state. Agriculture accounted for 31 per cent of Ireland's greenhouse gas emissions in 2016 (source: European Environment Agency). While the recession of 2008–12 helped, in absolute and relative terms, to reduce greenhouse gas (GHG) emissions the rate has been creeping back up. The agricultural and transport sectors stand out as major contributors to these outcomes. It does not have to be so: Denmark, for example, manages to keep a lid on GHG emissions through technologically efficient means in both of these sectors.

The extent of dependence on imported fossil fuel energy is of huge concern. CSO data confirm a rise in dependency from 69 per cent in 1990 to 88 per cent of all energy imports in 2015 with a significant switch from coal and oil to gas over this period (CSO, 2017). Eurostat measures energy dependency as net energy imports divided by the sum of gross energy consumption. The figure for the Republic of Ireland was 69.1 per cent in 2016 compared to 53 per cent on average for the EU28. Given the exceptionally high dependence by the Republic of Ireland on fossil fuel imports it is clear that patterns of consumption, production, energy use and importation must change urgently. A high dependence on fossil fuel imports not only exposes Ireland to supply volatility, but also to price hikes when events such as trade wars or political instability might suddenly impact supply.

A modest fall in total greenhouse gas emissions in the Republic of Ireland from a peak value of 127.4 in 2005 (base year 1990=100) to a level of 113.4 in 2016 is welcome but we must do better – especially as some of this fall was related to the 2008 disruption in economic activity (Figure 14).[42]

A sudden shock to the global economy arising from a hike in energy costs could have a disproportionate and destabilising effect on Irish economic conditions. While energy supplies may not necessarily be as constrained as feared some years ago due to the development of new sources through oil and gas finds off the Irish coast or through the development of new technologies and sources in other countries, the high dependence on imports of oil and gas is far from ideal. And although the development of nuclear power and shale extraction (fracking) have been cited as necessary alternative sources of energy in Ireland, the case for this has not been convincingly established given the environmental and other risks associated with such developments. Nuclear power stations are inflexible in their operations and therefore an unsuitable complement to renewable energy (Denny, 2014).

Investment in renewable energy is essential in order to diversify our energy sources, thus reducing exposure to external shocks as well as ensuring a more ecologically friendly form of energy consumption. However, the costs of investment in renewable energy are considerable and may have a negative impact on some communities, as in the establishment of inland wind turbines. Other systems of renewable energy are constantly evolving: solar panels, for example, have come down in price thanks to trade with China while onshore and offshore wind energy production faces lower cost barriers than a decade ago.

Future technological change may open up even safer, efficient and cheaper options. Investment in renewable energy is therefore an important component of a medium-term strategy – but it is not a panacea. Changes in climate with associated extreme weather events over the medium- and long-term will require additional investment in repair, adaptation and preventive measures. However, we need to be mindful of the possibility of the Jevons paradox whereby increased efficiency on the supply side serves to stimulate higher demand and thus cancels out the environmentally positive effects of production efficiency. The building of the M50 motorway around Dublin, for example, certainly took heavy traffic out of the city centre but it also stimulated car use around Dublin and that, coupled with the construction of hyper retail outlets strategically located at key junctions along the M50, has created a new set of traffic problems.

The European Union has agreed a target for renewables of 20 per cent in total energy consumption by the year 2020 with a sub-target of 16 per cent for the Republic of Ireland. While the share of renewables in 2016 at 9.5 per cent was well below the EU average of 17 per cent, the proportion of renewables in electricity generation in the Republic of Ireland was relatively close to the EU average (27 per cent against an EU average of 30 per cent) and was close to the EU transport average. The biggest shortfall occurs in the category of 'heating and cooling' (6.8 per cent against 19.1 per cent). Compared to Finland, for example, the Republic of Ireland is well behind on renewable energy we keep resources in all of the three key sectors.

The term 'circular economy' has been coined in recent times to refer to an economy in which we keep resources in use for as long as possible, the maximum value is extracted from them while in use, then products and materials are recovered and regenerated at the end of each service life. Linear or non-circular economy, by contrast, is oriented towards extraction of resources, production and disposal (O'Rafferty, 2017).

One possible measure of the extent to which we make efficient use of material resources is the resource productivity index. The index measures the ratio of GDP at constant prices to domestic material consumption (DMC): DMC refers to all material inputs extracted from the natural environment including bio-mass, metallic minerals, non-metallic minerals and fossil fuels plus 'net imports' of such materials.

Not surprisingly, the ratio of efficiency given by RPI (Figure 15) has improved over time, helped in part by the recession in construction. However, the surge in GDP in 2015 has had a significant impact on the measure of interest here. Following a sharp drop in GDP in 2009 a gradual recovery lead to an upturn in 2015 reflecting unusual and tax-avoiding corporate behaviour that year. DMC fell steeply following the crash of 2008 but has recovered since 2012. The role of the construction sector was significant during 2009–12 in pulling down DMC through its impact on the extraction of sand, gravel and crushed rock.

Figure 16 provides a European comparison: the Republic of Ireland fares better than most other EU states on this measure of productivity in use of materials consumed but the picture changes when the exceptional jump in GDP to a higher and inflated level is taken into account. The corrected value of RPI is probably lower than it is in most other EU states.

Is the Republic of Ireland becoming more efficient and are there grounds for hope in relation to a movement towards a more circular economy? The measurement of economic circularity is particularly challenging given the complex supply chains underlying construction and manufacturing (for example, dairy products).

The NESC report offers a relevant observation (O'Rafferty, 2017, p. 27):

> The circular economy would seem to offer a rationale for a fresh approach to an Enterprise Strategy for indigenous sectors focussed on clustering. This could increase the reliance on mainly local supply chains and provide resilience in the context of Brexit.

The Republic of Ireland has an overall better record than other EU member states in reducing reliance on landfill for municipal waste management (there is a landfill ban in some European countries). At just over 20 per cent of total municipal waste in the form of landfill in 2014, the Republic of Ireland could improve by aiming for below 5 per cent as is the case in Austria, Belgium, Finland, Germany, Netherlands and Sweden, all of which invest heavily in local alternatives such as material recycling and composting.

The prospects for international agreement and corresponding action to significantly reduce CO_2 emissions within the next ten years appear to be limited in spite of the growing evidence that such emissions will lead to an irreversible and disastrous rise in temperatures with global consequences. There is a moral imperative on all countries, including Ireland, to cooperate in this matter as well as address the underlying causes, which are political and moral as much as technological and financial in nature. While a totally decarbonised economy may not be feasible, rapid progress in the right direction is critical and the highest priority needs to be accorded to this goal.

A need for fundamental shifts in public policy

A new inter-generational understanding is vital to effectively distribute jobs, income and lifelong learning openings. With the island population heading towards 10 million in the latter half of this century, and with a dramatic environmental challenge, there is an urgent need to reconfigure transport connections and spatial planning.

Policies must also provide for social needs as our population ages. They must reflect the uncertainty around migration flows where a resumption of significant inward migration is likely given the shifting economic conditions and the long-term impact of climate change in other continents. A key part of the strategy will be to further increase the employment rate in the adult working population, measured as the percentage of 20–64-year-olds who are in employment as reported in the European Labour Force Survey. An increase in the standard retirement age of 65 (where circumstances require it) should be considered. Given higher life expectancy and revisions to the eligibility age threshold for the state pension planned in the future it will be important to expand, in some areas of the labour market, opportunities for voluntary extension of working life to beyond the age of 65, as is already the case in many sectors.

New technology and AI underline the need for workforce planning. Where jobs are displaced or changed, new opportunities must be sought in areas demanding skill, communications and personal care. A guaranteed standard of living with access to learning opportunities and more flexible pathways to retirement could ease the transition to a shorter working week but a longer working life where people wish to extend their time in the workforce.

The necessary large-scale and lasting change in consumer and producer behaviours required to meet environmental change cannot be achieved by nation states acting on their own. Neither will the scale and timeliness of change occur by means of changes in market incentives through a policy of mere enhanced regulation, taxation or subsidies – important as these are as part of a wider strategy. A greater role for states is required in setting prices, choking off fossil-fuel burning and investing in long-term renewable energy.

Living in a fast-changing world, we need to plan and to cooperate for a better future. The Democratic Programme of 1919 is still as relevant today as it was a hundred years ago. The context may be different but the values remain the same: essentially, that 'every citizen shall have opportunity to spend his or her strength and faculties in the service of the people'.

PART II

PROPOSALS FOR A
NEW ECONOMIC ORDER

5

Taking Work Seriously

The nature of work

Work defines us as human beings. The exercise of body and mind in the production of goods and services for sustenance and enjoyment gives meaning to our lives. An Ireland worth working for is one where work is taken seriously, not just as a means for people to survive and meet their basic needs outside the workplace but also as an end in itself. Work that is well paid and valued, respected and integrated into environments characterised by values of respect, democracy and equality contributes directly to an individual's sense of self-worth. As Chang (2014, p. 373) put it, 'without taking work more seriously, we cannot build a more balanced economy and a more fulfilled society'.

Many of the most important parts of human work are outside the paid labour market as measured by statisticians and economists. From caring for children to supporting the local community, a huge amount of time is expended outside the formal labour market. Love, care and solidarity are key motivators and rewards of work and yet receive remarkably little attention in the literature of economics. It is difficult to put a monetary value on this time but it is certain that without such work the economy, as measured by paid work, would cease to function. Unpaid work is no less economic in purpose and effect than paid work. For this reason, GDP (or other measures of total income and output in a country) is only a limited guide to total economic activity and even less to human well-being.[43]

The American feminist economist Nancy Folbre argues that from a statistical and national accounting point of view, treating caring labour as being outside economic activity had the effect of devaluing the economic worth of such work and distorted its contribution to general economic well-being (1994, p. 96):

> The point here is that the image of the unproductive housewife was connected to a cultural norm that portrayed women as dependents who should be grateful for their husbands' support. The devaluation of housework and child care was enforced by the official terminology of economists and statisticians.

A goal for any society is to enable all its citizens to provide for themselves the goods and the means to live a life that they value. Individual freedom, family and community bonds and civic rights and responsibility are vital and indispensable elements of human well-being. Research on the determinants of individual well-being place huge emphasis on the role of employment and strong interpersonal ties (Healy, 2005). The two are related: creating and sustaining employment that provides for human need and dignity must be a primary goal of any society focussed on the well-being of all its members. We should not define employment too narrowly as activity orientated towards paid work.

A traditional patriarchal model of employment has influenced both social policy and patterns of participation in the labour market. In the tax and social welfare area, the household is the typical unit of analysis and focus for the purpose of tax liability and assessment, while there is a strong emphasis on tax credits or universal social payments linked to stay-at-home parents.

Public debate in Ireland and the UK has been very much focussed on taxes, social benefits and public services but should also examine the importance of wages and profits and their share in national income as well as the persistence of wage inequality. The state cannot be expected to make all the effort in terms of reducing income or wage inequality via taxes and welfare. There is a role for large public and private organisations in setting norms on pay levels by limiting the ratio of top to bottom salary levels. This could be part of pay bargaining at company, sectoral or national level. Public organisations could develop a code of pay norms, which could be transferred over into the area of public procurement, adding leverage to the setting of these norms across the domestic economy.

Work is central to political economy

Some economists use the term 'human capital' to describe the quantity and quality of the workforce, which takes into account individual levels of experience, education and various aptitudes. Others refer to human resources or talent. Labour, as a factor of production, is different to all of these in so far as it cannot be appropriated.[44] Workers sell their services in an often very competitive labour market and as individuals they are vulnerable to exploitation as well as precariousness in conditions, pay and tenure of employment.

Conflict of interest between capital and labour was a key insight of Karl Marx and other contemporary socialists who saw this conflict as the main driver of social and political change, especially in the transition from capitalism to socialism. Trade unions sprang from a pre-capitalist craft-guilds era but grew rapidly during nineteenth century industrialisation. General trade unionism arose from the needs of different groups of workers, including unskilled occupations, to combine efforts and advance workers' interests. Class conflict involving trade union action as well as various political manifestations of the trade union movement has been a feature of capital-labour relations ever since the rallying cry of Marx and Engels, 'Workers of the world unite!' rang out in 1848.

At various points in history, class compromises have been achieved involving a coordinated approach to industrial relations as well as give and take in terms of pay, working conditions and, in more recent decades, taxation, welfare and other areas of social policy. The Republic of Ireland witnessed a particularly clear example of what is termed social partnership in the period 1987–2008.

Adequacy of working hours and pay together with provision of appropriate working conditions and entitlements to protection together with access to pensions, sick pay and paid leave are a vital concern to working households. Work still accounts for a huge proportion of people's lives and the income they derive from paid work accounts for most of household consumption and provides the basis for much of government revenue (whether through direct taxes on income from employment or indirectly on consumption, which is made possible by wages).

The relative neglect of all types of work, including its quality and accessibility, is a marked feature of recent political economy. Periodic elevated levels of unemployment and under-employment, especially among young adults, are regarded as inevitable and regrettable. The default position on the part of monetary and fiscal authorities is that these problems are not soluble except through long-term supply-side measures including labour market reforms to keep wages below certain levels and make hiring and firing easier. Evidence that this is the case is provided by the estimations made by economists (and enshrined into EU and domestic law) of the structural government deficit. Underlying these estimates is a broadly accepted consensus that unemployment rates approximately in the 4–7 per cent range are natural. The implication of this is that an economy with a 5 per cent unemployment rate could be said to be operating more or less at full capacity and any further stimulatory fiscal or monetary measures would be excessive and might contribute to economic overheating.

Missing from this consensus is an ethical perspective that acknowledges the profoundly demoralising and degrading impact of unemployment or under-employment, especially for those trapped in long-term spells of unemployment. One is left with the impression that some level of unemployment is 'necessary' as a means to tame the labour market, including wage claims, in a way that is reminiscent of an industrial reserve army of labour as referred to by Marx.

Competition is driven by price as well as quality of goods and resources. However, labour is a key ingredient in the efforts of enterprisers to survive and flourish. Labour, well managed and managing in a mix of diverse forms of ownership, can transform the capacity of enterprises to perform on global and local markets. Seen this way, labour is much more than a cost facing entrepreneurs: it is also a value and a vital source of productivity. This is all the more the case when labour becomes part of the ownership and management structure of an enterprise. We should never forget that, at a macro level, labour is a cost to enterprise as well as the source of demand for the goods and services produced in these enterprises.

Access to work

Since work is central to all economic activity, the quality and quantity of such work is a vital component of a vision for the future. Both the total numbers in paid work and the proportion of the whole adult population in paid work are relevant.

Typically employment is measured by the total number of persons at work according to rules agreed internationally by statisticians. Although difficult to measure precisely, the total number of hours of paid work is part of regular statistical publications on the labour market. Wages paid to workers are sometimes referred to as compensation, implying that a person's work is not particularly pleasant and that this person needs to be compensated for doing it. The stability and level of wage income is a vital concern for workers. But there is also a wide range of non-cash or near-cash returns to work that are crucial for workers and their families: provision of income when workers are sick, unemployed or taking time off work to undergo training or education are as important as wage income. In many European social insurance systems provision of such benefits is linked to people's employment history of contributions and paid into a special social insurance fund. Systems of social insurance have existed in the UK and the Republic of Ireland since the 1940s although they are less the focus of social policy than is the case in many large continental European countries such as France and Germany.

Unemployment or under-employment is a blight on individuals and whole communities because it robs people of their dignity, status and rights. It constitutes a waste and a social scandal when young people, in particular, are forced to seek work abroad or in sectors or occupations little suited to their education and aptitude. Under-employment, unemployment and precariousness of work has emerged as a new global phenomenon and appears to be long-lasting and embedded even when general employment conditions have improved.

A full-employment target is needed to complement the inflation target much beloved of central banks across the world. However, measuring price inflation is one thing; measuring full employment is another. Full employment is only very approximately measured with reference to the unemployment rate. Extensive pockets of under-employment, non-standard employment arrangements including casual, zero-hours or 'if-and-when' contracts and involuntary part-time work make it difficult for statisticians to measure the overall slack in the labour market. However, based on official labour market statistics we know that under-employment is, typically, at least twice the standard unemployment rate. Under-employment was in excess of 20 per cent in 2018 in the Republic of Ireland.[45] Using a separate statistical measure for Northern Ireland in 2018, NISRA report that 15 per cent of part-time workers would work more hours if those hours were available. Overall, 4 per cent were unemployed in Northern Ireland in 2018.

Some recent job gains have been short-term, precarious and badly matched to a highly skilled young workforce. Other employment gains have been in relatively highly paid and skilled positions dependent on footloose service industries located in Ireland for the time being. Sustainable employment implies flexibility and security. However, as Nugent (2017, p. 1) has pointed out, 'the incidence of involuntary part-time and temporary work is higher among low-skill workers'. Wilson (2017) has noted the specific gendered nature of insecure employment with the prevalence of a culture of uncertainty of hours, low pay and insecurity of contract higher in particular sectors such as hospitality and retail. The Irish Congress of Trade Unions (2017a) has recently charted the rise and spread of insecure work across the whole island of Ireland.

In any period, total employment includes a significant number of part-time workers as well as persons who may have taken up temporary positions or casual employment contracts depending on the timing of the survey. Some people prefer part-time hours for family, personal or other reasons. Others would like to work more hours but cannot due to lack of available working hours or the nature of their employment contract. Although limited in scale, the incidence of 'bogus self-employment' seems to have increased both in the UK and in the Republic of Ireland in recent times. This seems to be the case in certain sectors and among particular occupations. Bogus self-employment describes patterns of employment where, for the purposes of paying tax and social insurance as well as being recorded in statistical surveys, persons are returned as 'self-employed' but have all or many of the characteristics of being an employee. Such patterns of employment can be exploitive in that employers save on social insurance costs as well as other statutory related costs associated with having employees.

A combination of employment and training opportunities underwritten by the state is required especially during periods of economic downturn or long-term structural change such as might arise from Brexit and other international developments. Care is needed in how training opportunities are designed and linked to paid employment particularly in the light of experience with various 'workfare' (having to work while in receipt of public assistance) and unpaid internship interventions. Employment should be guaranteed by the state as a last resort where markets fail to provide full employment.[46] In order to be effective and consistent with human rights to dignity in work, a public job guarantee should be designed to match the needs, skills and circumstances of participants (there is no point, for example, in offering training to parents who have no access to childcare); offer a living income while participants gain experience and contribute to the social good; provide quality work experience and training to participants in such a manner as to equip them to find and secure employment following a period of participation in a scheme; not displace other workers by undercutting wage costs; and offer voluntary participation so that unemployed persons are not forced to take up employment.

The subject of guaranteed work is discussed and proposed as an area for policy action in the UK by Anthony Atkinson in his book *Inequality: What Can Be Done?* (2015). The idea is compatible with proponents of Modern Monetary Theory who argue that a central bank (such as the European Central Bank in the case of the Eurozone) can and should expand debt to absorb under-employed resources without risk of price inflation.

The case for higher employment rates is threefold:

- Under-employment and unemployment are hugely damaging to individuals, communities and societies.
- Demographic change in the coming two decades will require higher rates of participation in the labour market throughout the whole age span of 'working life' and beyond to include work-learning experience for young people and employment opportunities for those over the age of 65 who want and need to engage in paid work and have the skills to continue making a valuable contribution to organisations and communities.
- High employment rates are associated with a social capacity to provide quality public services and income protection to the most vulnerable.

Following a very welcome rise in employment rates from the 1990s onwards, rates for those in the 20–64 age group fell with the onset of the 2008 crisis (Figure 17). Male employment rates in particular took a heavy hit in 2008–12, reflecting the implosion of the construction sector.

What is most telling is the comparison with other Northern European countries where employment rates are well in excess of those in the Republic of Ireland. The Republic of Ireland is ahead of the EU28 averages for females and males, but these results provide no grounds for complacency. Figure 18 provides an overview of rates across individual EU28 members states in 2017. The Republic of Ireland is well behind a number of Northern European countries especially with regard to rates of female employment. This reflects, in a major way, the lack of affordable childcare.

If we aspire to levels of public service underpinned by higher levels of domestic productivity we must raise employment rates in the Republic of Ireland – especially among women – to a Scandinavian level. Contrasting a selection of Northern European countries or regions shows that both parts of Ireland lag behind other jurisdictions with regard to female employment rates (Figure 19).

A rate of 80 per cent among 20–64-year-olds should be considered a realistic target by the mid-2020s. An effective means of increasing and retaining female participation in the labour force is the provision of parental leave. In Sweden, for example, working parents may each avail of up to six months of parental leave at 80 per cent of sick pay levels. Three months of this allocation is not transferable.

Equality in the workplace

Various longitudinal data analyses indicate that increased total working time in the labour market for women has not been accompanied by a corresponding fall in household working time (Gershuny and Robinson, 1988). To increase employment rates and enhance the quality of working lives, we need to adapt working hours and arrangements. This will mean greater flexibility of paid working hours, a different allocation between men and women of caring work in the community and at home as well as a shift in lifestyle. Too often workers are under pressure to work long hours to make up a living wage or because of market pressure allied to a particular organisational culture. An expectation of long hours breeds inequality as well as undermining personal health – itself a key factor in productivity or lack of it.

Some sectors have made progress in limiting working hours as well as providing choice and flexibility to workers to help them balance paid work and other areas. The European Union has played a significant and positive role in promoting rights to parental leave and security of hours under particular conditions. Yet legal protection remains limited. At one extreme, when and if contracts along with zero-hour contracts undermine access to stable employment hours and a corresponding living income. At the other extreme, workers have excessive hours. This may be related to the nature of their contract (for example, junior doctors in public health) or to the pressure to make ends meet (such as in double-jobbers or workers in precarious employment in the hospitality, contract cleaning or fast-food business).

Russell, Maître and Watson (2016) have tracked and identified trends in work-related illness, suggesting the existence of a pro-cyclical pattern where physical and mental illnesses associated with work increase during times of economic downturn and fall during times of recovery.

Equality of treatment also applies to patterns of pay and promotion. There are marked differences in pay between men and women, brought about by a range of factors including differences in access to childcare, inherited culture and discriminatory attitudes and practices. The unadjusted pay gap provides a crude measure of differences in pay for employees in enterprises of ten or more workers. At a gap of 21 per cent, the Republic of Ireland lies towards the upper end on this measure in 2014 for the business economy (the latest year for which Irish data were available). By contrast, the gap was only 14 per cent in 'public administration'. It was 16 per cent in healthcare and 17 per cent in education (Figure 20).

Wages and poverty

The extent of wage inequality within companies in the Republic of Ireland is difficult to track but has been highlighted in a report by the Irish Congress of Trade Unions (2017b) as well as in a more recent work by Michael Taft (2018). Micheál Collins (2016) has estimated that, in 2014, there were approximately 70,000 workers – or 5 per cent of all employees – on the minimum wage, most of whom were women (73 per cent). Most were under the age of 40 and many were working in hospitality and retail sectors. While the causes of poverty are complex and there is much to be done to address the roots of poverty, it is clear that participation in employment and the level of wage-floor protection are relevant to an overall anti-poverty strategy.

Poverty is highly correlated with lack of access to employment. However, low pay and insecurity of working hours creates what is called 'in-work poverty'. To counter poverty at work many have championed the idea of a living wage, which some employers, notably in the UK, have taken up. A living wage is defined as a level of pay that enables an individual or family to live a life with dignity in a given culture and society. It is difficult to define a precise amount in terms of annual or hourly pay (assuming that pay is based on hours of work). Various research methods have been used to estimate a living income (and from there a living wage) based on different households types (for example, a single adult, or two adults and both working or two adults and two children and one adult working, etc.).[47]

The focus on living wage advocacy and research is on a single representative household type averaging across regions within a country. This is the approach taken by the Vincentian Partnership in the Republic of Ireland working in collaboration with a number of other organisations including the NERI.[48] It is necessary to avoid confusion by distinguishing between three distinct concepts or measures:

- The statutory National Minimum Wage (which was €9.55 of gross pay per hour for employees over the age of 18 and not in their first job in the Republic of Ireland in 2018).
- A household living income as measured by various research organisations based on an extensive study of household budgets and requirements.
- A 'living wage' narrowly defined as pay per hour for a single adult worker (set at €11.90 in the Republic of Ireland in 2018).[49]

Payment of a living wage as measured by hourly pay is one thing; a living income is another. The partner of a millionaire banker could work for ten hours a week at an hourly rate of pay of €10. This would place the latter individual in the category of working below a living wage. Similarly a teacher and lone parent could work for three hours a week for eight months of the year at an hourly pay rate of €35. This teacher might be living in acute poverty but earning three times the hourly living wage rate in the Republic of Ireland.

There are flaws and pitfalls in the debate on a living wage. The concept of a living wage might be reduced to gross pay per hour without considering the complex interaction between hourly wage rates, number of hours of work, taxation and social benefits and security of employment. Moreover, the importance of social wage corresponding to various entitlements or incomes during periods of retirement, ill health or parental leave needs to be considered. There is a risk that an exclusive focus on the statutory hourly wage rate or, indeed, the living wage, however defined and measured, may deflect attention from the overall level and adequacy of wages as well as its distribution. Taken to an extreme, a reductionist focus on the living wage rate could work against low-paid workers if it acted as a downward drag on wages towards a minimum level compatible with income adequacy.

Unfortunately, it is not possible to directly compare in-work risk of poverty in Northern Ireland with the Republic of Ireland. In-work poverty is defined, in the UK, with reference to 60 per cent of the median value of income 'before housing costs'. Typically, the household is the unit of analysis and in-work poverty relates to households with at least one individual member who is at work. On this measure, the proportion of all working-age adults in relative poverty was 20 per cent in 2013–14 compared to 15 per cent in 2006–07 (Figure 22).

Resetting labour market policy and practice

Radical changes in the labour market, technology and enterprises pose a huge challenge for trade unions everywhere, not only to hold to current levels of union density (the proportion of the workforce who are members of trade unions) but to reclaim ground lost in most countries since the mid-twentieth century. The strength and relevance of trade unions also matters greatly to young workers and to those about to enter the workforce. Where the delusion of choice, freedom and cost competitiveness has been spawned by low-cost business models we also find a significant long-term contributor to lower standards in the workplace.

The balance of power between capital and labour is relevant to a discussion of equality. In recent decades the balance between the rights of workers and those of employers or owners of capital has moved towards capital as rights to union action, bargaining and membership have been restricted in one country after another. This was particularly evident in the UK from the beginning of the 1980s as well as in the Republic of Ireland where trends in thinking and legislation were reflected in various legal innovations including, for example, the 1990 Industrial Relations Act. In the case of the Republic of Ireland there has been the additional feature of a provision on private property in its written constitution, which has been generally interpreted in a very restrictive way by the courts. Restrictions on the rights of labour as well as declining union density have gone hand in hand with increased income inequality in many jurisdictions. Public policies to pursue greater equality in the long run must include legal protections for organised labour.

The gradual dismantling or containment of labour rights needs to be addressed as part of a strategy to democratise workplaces and enhance the quality of labour. Stronger and more effective legislation will be required to enshrine rights to collective bargaining (supplemented if necessary by constitutional referendum) as well as protect rights to information, tenure and additional hours where available as well as a rooting out of bogus self-employment. Effective legislation should ensure that a repetition of the situation arising from the closure of Clery's department store in Dublin in June 2015 and the associated instant dismissal of workers could never happen again. Enforcement of labour rights needs to involve an adequately resourced inspection system covering all sectors and areas of the country.

Policies to lift workers out of low pay combined with progressively loaded pay increases and caps on very high earnings are urgently needed. Personal income tax is a powerful policy tool but cannot be the only one to address equality. As part of a pre-distribution policy agenda, it is necessary to enhance trade union capacity and rights to negotiate collectively for workers. The 2015 Industrial Relations (Amendment) Act has made cautious progress to this end. It would appear that a constitutional amendment is the only legally secure way of attaining full collective bargaining rights. Where trade unions are strong and effective, workers can restore lost ground in terms of the labour share of national income and narrow the gap between the highest paid and the lowest paid in organisations.

As more and more workers will continue to work into their sixties, a sensible approach is to give people choices and guarantees in relation to income. The option of working beyond the statutory commencement age for the state pension needs to be enshrined in rules, laws and collective agreements. In the face of advancing automation of processes in manufacturing and retail there must be scope for retraining of workers. It may also be possible to reduce paid working hours with no reduction in earnings. Other alternatives might include shorter working hours and earnings but with guaranteed employment for those who would prefer to opt for such arrangements especially in sectors where, up until now, family-friendly provisions have been limited or non-existent.

A reformed social insurance system would enhance labour market participation as it directly links benefits during periods of unemployment, sickness or parental leave.

Addressing the obstacles to lack of choice would require a number of initiatives including negotiation of flexible working time at local and national levels in the context of partnership negotiations; facilitation of greater mobility in and out of the labour market as well as flexibility in terms of working time; support, recognition and accreditation for alternating periods of caring, working, training; and gradually changing a culture that assumes that men are naturally the main breadwinners and women naturally the main carers.

A number of goals are worth striving for to counteract precarious work: stability and predictability of hours, limitations on excessive working hours, a guaranteed minimum number of hours and rights to time off or flexibility according to agreed social and sector-specific norms.

Here are four practical suggestions for realising those goals:

- raise the national gross hourly minimum wage to at least 60 per cent of the median in the business economy in both parts of Ireland by 2025;
- increase labour protection legislation, monitoring and enforcement in both parts of Ireland to outlaw exploitive or illegal job contracts;
- invest in upskilling and innovation: a target of 95 per cent NFQ level 5 (Leaving Certificate or equivalent) could be set for all adults by 2030 with a particular focus on a reformed

apprenticeship system and vocational further/higher education sector to raise skill levels to Levels 6 and 7 or higher for more than 70 per cent of all adults;

– raise workforce skills to a level of 60 per cent GCSE levels A–C or higher in Northern Ireland.

6

Raising the Social Wage

Striving for the good life

Until now I have treated the subject of work and wages associated with work. Next I will broaden the discussion of work and wages to include what I call 'the social wage', which I define as the resources and income received by people both in direct income (wages and social transfers) and public services such as education, healthcare, public transport and public housing.

A proper balance needs to be struck between public, private-for-profit and voluntary or non-public community initiative with regard to the provision of goods and services crucial to human well-being – for example, education, health, housing and key areas of economic infrastructure such as transport, broadband and energy. Recent decades have seen a sharp increase in private-for-profit medicine and education with the development of various commercial, for-profit service activities in schooling, vocational education, higher education, early childhood care, healthcare, elder care and other related areas. In many instances the service of teaching or personal healthcare is provided by a company or organisation operating in a market for such services.

Because education and health are so fundamental to human well-being and the continuing survival and development of societies, governments have taken a leading role in providing these services as well as funding them through general taxation. Whereas in the distant past such services were largely provided on a philanthropic or religious basis, public authorities have increasingly stepped into the role of provider, funder and regulator, especially from the nineteenth century onwards. Education and health were seen as public goods requiring public support and direction. In the case of education, the projects of teaching and raising skills were often tied up with the development of national consciousness and identity.

Retaining education and health as public goods provided to all without direct user charge is a worthy value and goal. They are under increasing pressure from commodification and user-charging. The provision of education and health forms one of the last frontiers in the effort to complete the neo-liberal project.

Central to a vision of social equality is access to quality childcare and education in the community. This is good for children and it is good for parents. It also addresses the obstacles to greater and continuing participation by women in the paid workforce. However, a quality childcare service presupposes proper funding and training for staff as well as flexible workplaces and adequate wages to allow parents to balance paid working time and caring for families.

The role of the state in developing key utilities (notably the Electricity Supply Board (ESB) in the 1920s) as well as initiatives in sectors such as rail transport, housing, life assurance, credit, telecommunications, forestry and natural resources was a feature of the post-World War II period. The neo-liberal project saw large segments of publicly owned commercial enterprises privatised in stages from the 1980s onwards, beginning with the opening up of markets to tendering and competition followed by the formation of publicly quoted companies on the stock exchange, leading to a partial sale of equity to private investors. The final stages of privatisation involved a complete sell-off of shares allegedly in the best interests of consumer and worker.

Making poverty history

The biblical saying that 'the poor shall always be with you'[50] has sometimes been misused either to justify inequality or material poverty measured in absolute terms. Poverty is not inevitable. Where there is a will there is way to reduce and even abolish. It begins and finishes with work: all types of work. Work is the key to generating sustainable income and self-reliance. Well-paid and skilled work is the key to reducing and abolishing in-work poverty. Allied to a comprehensive social insurance model to protect incomes during times of illness, parental obligations, study or retirement, work provides the basis for trust and consensus in sharing risks and enabling people to contribute their best as well as share in the cost of a new social bargain.

Work is the best means for people to avoid or exit poverty provided that (i) work is available, (ii) work pays an adequate income, and (iii) work is accompanied by a range of public services or goods accessible to all.

Pensions

Pensions are a form of deferred income. Throughout our working lives we put aside money to pay for our income in retirement in several ways, such as payment of general taxes (income, VAT and excise) to pay for old age pensions now and in the future; payment of social insurance towards an individual right to a contributory old age pension later in our lives; payment of a regular sum of money from our wages, which is treated as part of an occupational pension scheme; and savings of a regular or periodic sum of money from our income to go towards long-term needs including pension income.

In addition to periodic payments many of us benefit from one-off windfalls such as inheritance and gifts, which may or may not be significant at a particular stage in life. It is not uncommon, for example, that persons in the latter half of their working lives to benefit from an inheritance that goes towards a reduction in mortgage debt or investment in some asset to cover future needs.

Occupational pension schemes take two forms – defined benefit schemes and defined contribution schemes. Defined benefit (DB) schemes, which were more widespread in the past, are typically used in large enterprises including semi-state commercial enterprises. They define the benefit that members will receive on retirement (or death in the case of surviving partners and children). The risk is, in principle, borne by the employer. This is true when DB schemes are financially solvent, but long-term change such as the yield on safe assets in which pension funds are invested, changes in life expectancy and changes to minimum funding standards can impact dramatically on the solvency of schemes. Added to this is the extent to which companies can or are willing to pay for pensions by means of their contributions, which form part of total labour cost.

Defined contribution (DC) schemes have been growing in size in recent times. As the name suggests, DC schemes define the contribution of the employer and the employee but do not define the benefit. In effect, the entire risk is transferred to the employee.

The distinction between DB and DC schemes should not be confused with the distinction between end-of-career and career-average pension schemes. End-of-career pension entitlements are calculated on the basis of final salary in the year or years prior to retirement while career-average pension entitlements are calculated on the basis of average lifetime earnings. Given the impact of wage inflation and other factors, career-average pensions are much inferior to end-of-career pensions. This applies especially to women because they are more likely to have had interruptions to their earnings in the course of their working lives. In recent times some workers, including new entrants to the Irish public service since 2013, have been incorporated into a career-average pension scheme (referred to as the Single Public Service Pension Scheme) instead of end-of-career schemes. This will make a big difference not only to the cost of public services in the long run but to the incomes after retirement of those entering the public service in recent years.

It is unavoidable that many are not in a position to engage in paid work on a full-time basis either on grounds of age, caring responsibilities or mental or physical capacity. The state has an important role in assisting individuals and families not on the basis of some last-resort philosophy or on a patronising merit system. Every citizen and participant in society has a right to work and to a decent income. Social welfare payments constitute an important element of household income in the absence of which poverty would dramatically worsen.

Universal basic income

The notion that all citizens (or residents in a given jurisdiction) have an automatic right to a basic and living income to enable them to live with dignity and participate in a meaningful way is attractive. A universal basic income (UBI), advocated by some, would give every adult resident or citizen a basic flat rate of income from the state, regardless of age or labour market circumstances. This taxation-funded payment would correspond to an essential or living income and would be supplemented according to dependent children, disabilities and so forth. It is claimed that a simplification of the welfare system along these lines would reduce administrative and other social costs associated with an extremely complex welfare code. Pitched at an adequate level, a UBI could remove the scourge of poverty, but it is open to criticism: where has it worked successfully up to now and how much would it cost? These are relevant questions to which no satisfactory answers have so far been given.[51]

The implementation of a UBI is often proposed as part of a response to AI and its impact on certain jobs. A UBI also acknowledges the role of various unpaid forms of work, including caring. Properly managed and applied, a UBI could simplify systems of welfare eligibility assessment as well as provides a springboard for many to engage in positive social action outside the paid labour market undertaking new social or commercial enterprise ventures.

However, a possible consequence of a UBI without a wider social and economic transformation would be a reinforcement of inequality and a further rise in precarious work. Who decides what a living income is? Could there be inexorable pressure to reduce wages and social transfers to a common minimum level, removing many of the existing supports and protections that exist for vulnerable citizens? And how would citizens of other jurisdictions resident here fare, whether as refugees or economic migrants?

A key challenge to existing systems of social welfare is the assessment of needs in different individuals and households. It may be possible to define a living income or minimum expenditure standard for a given household type and make-up (e.g. two adults with two teenage children and living in a large city), but circumstances and needs vary hugely. What if one of the children has significant learning needs? What if rental costs of accommodation are three times the national average in the capital city? Such variations could be reflected in an adjustment to the UBI, which would make it look like modern-day social welfare systems.

Some analysts go so far as to suggest that a UBI could lead to the abolition of the national minimum wage (where such exists) so that anyone could work for any wage since their basic income is guaranteed (Wright 2013, p. 21). The challenge in practical terms of such an approach is that it refocuses the question of income distribution away from the power relationship between labour and capital to the role of the welfare state in undertaking a redistribution of income and transfers.

Throughout this book, I am strongly emphasising the role of work. The best way to tackle poverty is to secure jobs and wages that pay. State initiative and policies have a critical role in protecting those on low income as well as advancing pro-equality policies but ultimately it is workers organised in trade unions and in associated political activity who hold the key to the goal of making poverty history.

Universalism or means-tested?

Should services and interventions be targeted at the poor (some might, revealingly, say the deserving poor) or should services be provided on a universal basis? The argument for targeting services and payments is that they provide better and more efficient use of scarce public resources. Why should particularly expensive services such as public funding of medical education be so heavily subsidised when some of its beneficiaries could pay more of the costs upfront or pay back the cost through a student loan system? And why would all health services be provided free at the point of usage to people over a certain age regardless of their income and wealth? The case for universalism is challenged not only on the grounds of public affordability but on the grounds of fairness.

Counterbalancing these arguments is the case for universal goods and services in providing a seamless and less bureaucratic way of delivering shared goods. Everyone benefits in some way, and not just those directly consuming a service or in receipt of a particular payment. There is, however, another side of the coin: extensive use of means-testing for eligibility creates a 'them and us' society where some people are prone to resentment about having to pay for others (described as living off welfare or do not work). There is every possibility that a move away from universalism greatly risks reinforcing resentment and eroding a collective sense of responsibility and mutuality. The creation of the National Health Service (NHS) in post-war and debt-crushed Britain in 1948 met with fierce resistance from conservative and insider interests just as the limited proposed Mother and Child scheme did in 1950–51 in the Republic of Ireland. Many problems aside, the NHS has been a universally recognised success, becoming a constitutive element of British national identity. Universalism is costly but helps create an ethos of collective responsibility and rights and thereby helps sustain a wider social cohesion.

Universalism does not necessarily imply the creation of a welfare state or a nanny state in which freedom and choices are limited and people are incentivised to live off others. Well-designed systems of universality can coexist with a culture of agency and reward. For example, someone who loses a job might be eligible for relatively generous income protection while they undergo quality training for a new job on the understanding that the *additional* income support tapers off or disappears after a set period of time. The flip side of universalism in social payments and services is universalism in the payment of taxation: the notion that anyone can be exempt from the payment of taxation on income or property because of some status or occupation is not acceptable. However well intentioned, the decision to grant income tax exemption to artists in the Republic of Ireland in 1969 is not justifiable if we adhere to a principle that all should pay their fair share of tax in accordance with their ability to pay. If there is a case for public investment in the arts and encouragement of particular art forms then resources should be channelled to the appropriate infrastructure, development and assistance towards the exercise of creative work.[52]

Likewise, the decision to exempt or relieve very significantly particular corporations or high-wealth individuals is not justifiable for the same reason. The notion that a large number of individuals and households should be entirely exempt from income tax is questionable. While the income tax system serves to redistribute income it also pays for public services. On the principle that everyone should pay some amount, no matter how small, it should be accepted that even those on very low income should pay a modest amount of tax on income. This could be best done, as in some other European countries, by means of a pay-related social insurance contribution, which gives specific and clear individual entitlements to those paying.

A plan for homes

Ireland is facing a housing emergency. Following decades of under-investment in social housing allied to the impact of poor planning and inappropriate lending, a property-led speculative bubble burst in 2008 with disastrous consequences for hundreds of thousands of citizens. Profit-driven investment put speculative financial gain before the needs of people for a home. The delayed consequences of the volatile Irish property 'development' model became increasingly evident, as general economic conditions began to improve from 2013 onwards, in rising homelessness, a crisis of accommodation affordability and a chronic lack of housing supply. Government initiatives and announcements from 2014 onwards have yet to stem the escalating crisis.

The crisis in public housing supply has not been as acute in Northern Ireland although the implosion in the construction sector in the Republic of Ireland in 2008 and the years immediately following have taken their toll.

A roof over one's head and a safe, comfortable and healthy place that can be called home is a fundamental human right. Just as the issue of land was a central social concern and point of conflict in nineteenth-century Ireland, the question of accommodation was central to the social movement associated with the rise of trade unionism in the early years of the last century. Much of the social protest movement in both parts of Ireland during the late 1960s was related one way or another to housing.

An extraordinary feature of what came to be known as the Celtic Tiger period is that huge distortions were created in the supply of housing with inappropriate supply by type, cost and location. Not enough apartments were built in the right places while low-density sprawl was generated in locations poorly connected to urban centres or other towns. The inflation in prices across the country, especially in urban centres, lead to unsustainable patterns of lending and risk exposure. The market was misled by inappropriate tax breaks and other incentives. The principle of leaving housing almost entirely to the market with a dwindling share of public housing supply has stored up huge social problems now that the results of this long-term shift in policy are evident.

The Republic of Ireland moved from a heavily socialised component to housing in the 1940s to a much more significant share of private housing output in the 1980s. A combination of fiscal crisis in the mid-1980s coupled with the rising tide of neo-liberal economics in Irish public policy during the same period saw a big cutback in social housing output. Normal and long-term output levels were never restored. The economic crisis of 2008–12 was the final blow with an almost complete cessation in public supply. Coupled with a surge in private rental costs in recent years, this has had a catastrophic effect on individuals and families. The cost to the state in providing, among other things, short-term emergency accommodation, is significant. The approach of public policy before and after the collapse of the housing market in 2008–12 has been centered on market-led solutions including public subsidisation of private landlords and the promotion of public private partnerships (PPPs). The social and economic value of PPPs has been heavily and justly criticised by many including Hearne (2011).

Out-of-control rents are bad for everyone and must be addressed with suitable rental price caps. But the problem is essentially one of supply, with an under-investment in suitable housing in the right places by public and private enterprises. There is a vast backlog of demand for living accommodation, especially in the main urban centres. Demographics are a key driver of change with a rising population of younger persons seeking accommodation. A key concern is not only the cost of renting living space but tenure as well as predictability of rental costs. This is a huge burden for many families and individuals – especially those on low or unpredictable income due to precarious employment or unpredictable hours of work. (Nugent, 2018 and Turnbull, 2018).

A European cost rental model similar to that in use in Austria (Goldrick-Kelly and Healy, 2017) would distribute the cost of new homes over a long period of time and would socialise the costs of constructing and renting high-quality accommodation. A key feature of this model is the development of a much stronger rental sector with a mix of household types and incomes. To be effective and sustainable, the model would have to be self-financing in the medium term following an initial start-up phase where exchequer funding or injections of public and private capital would be necessary.

To increase the supply of housing to a level that meets aggregate housing demand as well as socially affordable demand within the aggregate, the NERI has proposed a single, unitary, mixed-income rental model operated by a commercial, publicly owned company and operating on a full cost-recovery basis. To achieve this, the NERI has also proposed the establishment of The Housing Company of Ireland (HCI) – a new entity to supplement and strengthen investment in social housing by local authorities.

The HCI would operate separately from the existing but reformed Housing Finance Agency (HFA), which would provide funding mainly to the HCI but also, where appropriate, to housing associations and local authorities as well as municipal housing associations established by the latter. All lending would be undertaken according to sound and verifiable criteria taking advantage of exceptionally low current interest rates on capital markets and drawing on the considerable reserves of equity and cash at the National Treasury Management Agency as well as the reputation and market access of the latter on international capital markets.

The funding base for an emergency housing programme to be undertaken by the HCI could be made up of a number of components, including the Irish Exchequer, the Irish Strategic Investment Fund, the European Investment Bank and other EU funding institutions, a new Irish Housing Solidarity Bond (e.g. for long-term pension investment) as well as domestic and international financial agencies including trade unions, credit unions and other civic organisations with capital.

An initial injection of €3 billion directly from the Strategic Banking Corporation of Ireland (the successor to Anglo-Irish Bank) to HCI could be leveraged by a lending flow of €9 billion (three times the equity injection) through the existing HFA to the HCI. The company would commission new housing directly through private companies, local authorities or existing approved housing bodies The aim is not to replace the existing social housing building activity of the local authorities, which is in any case at an all-time low and crippled by lack of finance. The proposed company could channel funding to local authorities to scale up social housing activity. Rental payments would service the cost of debt, construction and maintenance as well as provision for contingencies and upkeep.

Among the HCI's responsibilities would be the development of a comprehensive public register of land that would be rezoned for development. In this regard, the proposed company could incorporate the newly established Land Development Agency. The public and policymakers have a right to know what land is available, who owns it, approximately how much it is worth at current market values and what evaluations have been undertaken with regard to the suitability of such land for building, as well as relevant data on local public services (schools, health centres, transport, sports and other community facilities).

However, the HCI would not, without supplementary action by government, be in a position to close down the deadly loop of land hoarding in expectation of price increases driving even more land hoarding. Urgent action is needed at government level to freeze the price of development land at a maximum level above agricultural land price. Active land management policy linked to taxes on vacant sites and a long-term strategic plan is required.[53]

Finally, there is no reason why the HCI could not operate, on a commercial basis and in consort with the Housing Executive in Northern Ireland, where new housing output is required to meet rising population. Although the problem of housing affordability is not as acute in Northern Ireland as in the Republic of Ireland, it is a problem in particular areas, such as Belfast and the surrounding localities, and impacts on younger age cohorts (Mac Flynn and Wilson, 2018).

A plan for healthcare

Health of mind and body is a fundamental human right. Access to health services on the basis of need rather than ability to pay is a vital human need and right. The 1919 Democratic Programme asserted that 'it shall be the duty of the Republic of Ireland to take such measures as will safeguard the health of the people and ensure the physical as well as the moral well-being of the Nation'. The views of the *Report of Oireachtas Committee on the Future of Healthcare* (Houses of the Oireachtas, 2017a) are significant, especially in its statement of first principles, which calls for 'a vision and a plan for re-orienting the health service towards a high quality integrated system providing care on the basis of need and not ability to pay.'

The report (hereafter referred to as the *Sláintecare Report*) marks an important milestone as it represents a broad political consensus on the need to move away from a two-tier system of health provision in the Republic of Ireland to one based on need and funded mainly or almost entirely from public sources. Given the historical legacy of failure to deliver sufficient reform in the way healthcare is managed and funded, a political momentum to achieve a publicly funded, single healthcare system within a decade is to be welcomed. However, two significant matters need to be addressed: (i) There are areas of healthcare resource allocation and usage where improvements in performance could be achieved and further cost savings effected. Key examples of this include education in healthy living and investment in primary and comprehensive healthcare facilities; and (ii) any significant and continuing increase in health spending will require additional revenue. A working paper published by the NERI (Goldrick-Kelly and Healy, 2018) builds on the work of the *Sláintecare Report* while addressing these two areas.

Significant strides forward in healthcare and in health outcomes have been achieved over recent decades. Life expectancy has risen significantly while the Republic of Ireland is now above the European Union average on this measure (Figure 23). However, the close tie between social class background and health has not narrowed and there is a clear correlation between social class and health status (Figure 24).

In any jurisdiction, the provision of a quality and efficient health service entails the outlay of anything between 5 and 15 per cent of GDP, depending on many factors, including the level of development of a country. How expenditure for health is funded is a matter of societal and political choice. In common with most European countries the level of subvention from the state accounts for the bulk of expenditure in the Republic of Ireland. The Republic of Ireland has an unusual funding arrangement for the following reasons:

– The extent of out-of-pocket and private health insurance expenditure is greater than in other EU states.
– User charges have increased significantly in recent years (e.g. prescription re-imbursement limits, charges per item for medical-card holders and other charges have risen as a result of cutbacks in public spending on health).
– Investment in an integrated and adequately funded primary healthcare system remains patchy compared to other Northern European countries.

The Republic of Ireland maintains a strongly reinforced two-tier health system with access and timeliness of treatment or diagnosis rationed on the basis of access to private health insurance, which itself has become much more expensive in recent years.

Significant cutbacks to front-line services and supports such as home help and closure of hospital wards have had a knock-on cost effect, including emergency department admissions. Quality and timeliness of interventions have improved in some areas (e.g. cancer screening) but others (e.g. child and adolescent mental health services) remain dramatically underfunded and inadequate for a modern, economically developed country.

It might be more accurate to describe the arrangement concerning healthcare access as a three-tier one with approximately one in five adults not eligible for a medical card but not members of a private health insurance scheme (whether on grounds of affordability or choice). Waiting times for admission to hospital on an in-patient or outpatient basis vary markedly for the three main groups.

Is the Republic of Ireland spending more than it needs on health than elsewhere? The answer is complicated. Several factors come into consideration, including the age structure of population, the geographical spread of population (many health centres and hospitals in more dispersed populations cost more in per capita terms) and what is counted as health spending according to international statistical rules. Real spending on healthcare per capita is lower in the Republic of Ireland than in comparable Northern European countries (Figure 25). There are also significant differences among countries when it comes to the share of private spending. The Republic of Ireland is one of those where a combination of private health insurance payments, out-of-pocket health spending and GP costs make up a significant amount of spending.

In common with health systems elsewhere in Europe, over 50 per cent of the public health budget is consumed by wages and salaries. Given the nature of healthcare, staff are likely to be more highly educated, on average, than elsewhere in the labour force. Specialists and medical staff are paid in line with historical as well as cross-country patterns, especially in the English-speaking world. Care is needed in comparing salaries and conditions, given the wide variation in circumstances as well as differences in the cost of living and the social wage in different countries. The scope in the short term for effecting economies in public health spending is limited due to the demand-led nature of much of healthcare as well as the fixed nature of labour costs, which account for just more than half of total spending. That said, there may be some scope for economies, over time, especially in the following areas:

- effective health promotion and disease prevention;
- strategic investment in quality primary community healthcare to reduce the number of hospital referrals and unnecessary long-term and costly hospital stays;
- measures to better manage existing health facilities and reduce overlap, waste and bureaucracy;
- a transition to a single-tier, public health system and an end to private health in public hospitals, which is a form of cross-subsidisation of private patients by tax-paying public patients.

A universal healthcare system modelled on European lines would remove all or nearly all out-of-pocket expenditures. Three features of such a system would be breadth of coverage (all of the population and not just those eligible under means-tested criteria), scope (covering the full scope of health services from cradle to grave) and depth (covering all costs with minimal or no user charges).

What matters is how healthy people are and how long they live; in other words, the ratio of outcomes to spend and not the size of the spend itself. Healthy outcomes are a product of many factors, including diet and lifestyle and not just how many medical staff and facilities are available. But resources are important and availability of experienced staff as well as timely access to screening, diagnosis and intervention save lives and improve health outcomes. There is evidence that we need to spend more on some areas of health and spend it differently across others – as well as spend it more efficiently. It is unlikely that we can reduce the overall level of spending.

A plan for public transport

The amount of time spent not only in workplaces but in commuting and in unpaid work off-site needs to be addressed. Better public transport and better spatial planning could provide long-term solutions to excessive commuting times.

Planning and development need to work with the grain of the natural and social environment. The consequences of bad planning are evident in low-density urban sprawl coupled with inadequate public services, public transport, parks and access to green spaces. The environmental crisis challenges public policy to take bold and imaginative steps to encourage more and more people to abandon their cars and use public transport and other means to travel to work but this is only possible with a well thought-out and planned public transport network: a legacy of 'ribbon development' (one-off housing scattered across the landscape) in much of the Irish countryside has not advanced planning and the efficient use of transport and other public utility provision. A gradual switch to public or ecological transport means shifting the balance of incentives from the motor car to the train, bus, light-rail or other options such as cycling or walking.

An efficient and affordable system of public transport is the best incentive for people to get out of their cars and into more environmentally sustainable transport options. The true costs and benefits of public transport should be reflected in the pricing structure with a recognition of the difficult-to-measure benefit of a community-friendly transport system that connects communities, students and workers. Investing in a European-level public transport system also includes the need to address the energy mix: it is entirely realistic to plan for a progressive de-carbonisation of public transport with greater use of electricity and biomass fuels.

A new approach to spatial planning is called for that enables people to live closer to public services and places of work. This latter approach will require greater population density in urban areas but supported by sufficient green spaces and adequate and well connected public services and commercial outlets.

A plan for learning

Education should not be confused with schooling or training, however essential the latter are to any functioning modern society. Education encompasses *all* types of learning extending throughout the entire lifecycle. But lifelong learning does not refer solely to those forms of learning that occur after school or after college. However, continuing education and training in the Republic of Ireland is not as well developed as it is in northern European countries.

Families are the first and most significant communities in which learning takes place: Skills relating to speech, communications, getting on with others and learning how to do different things are learned in this setting and reinforced and developed in the more formal setting of childcare and schooling. The role of lifelong learning – including the development of workers' learning movements (that is, associations set by trade unions or by independent worker groups) – played a key role in the economic and social transformation of Scandinavian countries in the nineteenth century (Lakey, 2017).

We spend much of our adult life in paid or unpaid employment of one sort or another and acquire technical or vocational skills on the job as well as 'off the job' in institutions or organisations of education. The notion of apprenticeship training is associated with craft work and dual training but has a wider resonance when formal instruction, theory learning and reflection is interwoven into professional or skilled practice. The ancient Chinese saying 'Tell me and I forget, show me and I remember, let me do and I understand' draws on ancient wisdom and human experience. A properly functioning formal education and training system encompasses:

- heavy investment in the early years to lay the foundations of literacy, numeracy and other general skills and to enable children to learn how to learn and grow into young adults with increasing responsibility for their own learning;
- a link to applied learning in the classroom and beyond, challenging learners to take responsibility for their understanding and practice (this approach to learning has particular relevance during the teenage years, which coincide with secondary-level education);
- a strong framework of support, training options and qualifications for adults as they develop different needs, interests and capacities.

A rebalancing of expenditure would not necessarily mean spending less on higher education but it would mean putting in place resources to enable children to develop at a very early stage. This is particularly vital in the case of children disadvantaged as a result of family or socio-economic circumstances.

Learners continue learning to work and live with others in an ethical and responsible way and take responsibility for their own learning and actions, enabling the development of creativity and imagination as well as critical thinking.

An 'inside-out' system of education would mean more empowerment of learners to apply their learning in the workplace and in communities. This does not necessarily mean, for example, extending formal apprenticeship training to everyone at second level: it could mean shifting the emphasis away from formal, examination-focussed digesting of facts and theorems to learning that is more practice-based and that prepares people to use social tools such as language, mathematics and science.

Early childhood care and education (ECCE) has received much public attention in recent times. From a haphazard and poorly coordinated private service offering a mixture of adapted for-profit facilities in people's homes to more commercially-run centres with accredited staff and ancillary services including after school care, the system of ECCE has grown in an unplanned and uneven way. The main challenge in this area confronting parents is cost: the service is expensive by international standards, reflecting the relatively low level of public subvention in spite of significant recent funding provisions (with some announcements in Budget 2017 in the Republic of Ireland stalled or delayed).

What is required is a national service with proper levels of staffing, accreditation, accompanying facilities suitable for young children and meaningful levels of inspection and accountability. A policy approach relying on tax credits or grants is likely to be wasteful and inefficient insofar as it does not address issues of cost, quality and accessibility. A publicly-provided service through local authorities as is done in many other OECD countries would provide a more suitable and effective solution: this could be complemented by a range of providers depending on local initiative and needs. To realise a full national ECCE service providing for two years of full-session care of twenty or more hours a week aimed at children in the 2–4 age group will involve a significant initial outlay of investment in appropriate facilities. In addition, the current costs of providing such a service, given age-appropriate necessary staff-to-child ratios is likely to cost at least half a billion euro in the case of the Republic of Ireland.[54] Objections to the cost of such a policy approach on the grounds of tight public finance constraints must be weighed against the reality that total tax take in the Republic of Ireland is well below that of comparator countries[55] in the European Union.

Part of the reason families are under severe financial pressure is that public services are inadequate. The direct 'out-of-pocket' cost of education, early childhood care, health and others services are very high by international standards. A fairer and more economically efficient solution is to bring ECCE within the ambit of a national programme and service with well-trained staff and excellent facilities suitable for young children.

Educational equality enables people with exceptional talent to progress and to contribute to economic innovation and productivity. By contrast, an educational system that reproduces inequality through selection or managed intake of different groups is a hindrance to economic and social development – quite apart from the ethical and social desirability of giving every young person an equal chance and access to learning. Finland provides an example of how high standards of literacy and numeracy are attained in combination with an approach that favours equality of opportunity and outcome.

The challenge of new technologies, including AI, has been discussed earlier but an answer to these challenges lies in training, retraining and adaptability. The *Programme for the International Assessment of Adult Competencies* (PIAAC) was undertaken across OECD countries in 2012 as well as in Northern Ireland for which a special report was released in 2013. The PIAAC 2012 data are still the latest available on international comparisons of literacy, numeracy and problem-solving. Figure 26 provides a focus on numeracy skill levels for 25–34-year-olds – an important indicator or proxy of likely skill levels as younger age-cohorts replace older cohorts over time. The data suggest that both parts of Ireland have some way to go to raise adult skill levels.

Some analysts have noted a growing polarisation in the labour market as clerical and administrative occupations lose employment share to lower-skill and higher-skill occupations. This hollowing out of the middle of the workforce is driven, in part, by technology and has huge implications for particular sectors and groups. One way to respond to these changes is to retrain and refocus groups at risk in order to equip workers to deal with new technologies in newly emerging sectors. A combination of 'soft' social skills and adaptation to new technologies would provide a partial solution: an example of this might include development of skills in relation to care of the elderly where care staff who visit people in their own homes could avail of new technology to identify health needs or emergencies. Service sector jobs will increasingly require greater use of new technology as well as strong inter-personal skills.

The People's Fund

A better name for a rainy day fund is a People's Fund, which could be expanded to subsume the existing social insurance fund with a threefold remit: pay for specific benefits covered by an expanded pay related social insurance system; provide a temporary shock absorber to maintain public investment and income support where GDP falls by more than 2 per cent in a year (as it did in each of the three years 2008–10); and invest in long-term strategic projects in areas of social housing, public transport and renewable energy.

A number of 'known' and 'unknown' developments must be considered in planning the use of public resources to the middle of the century. As Irish society ages there will be pressure to spend more on pensions and health. At the same time, high birth rates in the Republic of Ireland experienced over the last two decades will exert considerable pressure on demands for educational spending over the next two decades.

Ireland is also under pressure to reduce the use of fossil fuels and the carbon content of its transport, agriculture, home heating, electricity production and manufacturing activities. A radical change in patterns of consumption and production will require decades of sustained investment in renewable energy, public transport and energy-saving measures. Alongside this, taxes on 'bads' (that which pollutes or causes harm to health) will need to be raised to pay for investment in sustainable forms of economic activity and public investment in renewables.

There will be future financial shocks. Public support to banks in trouble will arise in the coming decades. The history of public bailouts of banks did not end with the advent of a limited and small-scale European Stability Mechanism in 2014. Other shocks arising from climatic and political influences and completely unforeseen developments are bound to arise. A People's Fund created with the apportionment of a fixed percentage of GDP would target bottlenecks and infrastructural deficits. Rather than seeing it as dead money put aside in the event of an emergency (rather like what a household might do), governments should invest more and better to equip us to meet future challenges, known and unknown.

Four short-term policy targets

There is a link between under-investment in the social wage and what may be popularly understood as the cost of living (Figure 27). The Republic of Ireland stands out as having a relatively high cost of living, although a number of Scandinavian countries share the same plight. What is particularly striking about the more detailed breakdown of price differences in 2017 (and available on the Eurostat website) is the relatively high cost of housing (including fuel, gas and electricity), health services as well as alcohol and tobacco. The price index values (EU28=100) are housing (148), health (160), tobacco (208) and alcohol (167). The following is proposed:

- Increase government revenue in the Republic of Ireland to at least 45 per cent of modified national income by 2025.
- Begin a stepwise increase in social insurance in the Republic of Ireland over a ten-year period to reach EU norms to pay for pensions and income during periods of reduced participation in the labour market. The first step should include a targeted increase in employer social insurance contribution in respect of earnings by the top 10 per cent of wage earners.
- Ring-fence public capital investment in the Republic of Ireland to 4 per cent of national income to ensure adequate investment in social and economic infrastructure.

-   In Northern Ireland use whatever limited revenue raising discretion exists to reform local property taxes to pay for local infrastructural projects, including investment in alternative energy sources.

7

Taxes – the Price of a Civilised Society

Fostering a high-productivity and high-skill economy so that we can pay for public services and share the fruits of prosperity is key to tax reform. The Institute for Public Policy Research Commission on Economic Justice (IPPR, 2018, p. 23) concluded that 'Higher taxes bring better quality public and social goods and greater levels of social cohesion, and the trust which goes with them'.

The capacity of any society to resource housing, health, education and other key services relates to taxation. Clearly there are limits to what the state can and should provide by way of direct transfers to make up or supplement people's income or provide education, health and other care. A balance must be struck between different wants, which are infinite, and resources, which are finite.[56] That balance has altered over time. From a heavy reliance on families, local communities and various charitable or religious institutions, provision of income and care moved strongly into the realm of state responsibility in the course of the twentieth century. Taxation levels increased significantly over much of the first half of the last century to match this in the major economies, spiking with the cost of two world wars and their aftermath. A strong reaction to this trend, however, set in from the late 1970s onwards.

This chapter explores different aspects of the tax system with reference to the Republic of Ireland. The level, distribution and nature of taxation and associated public spending in the case of Northern Ireland is complex and would necessitate a separate discussion.[57]

A poor 'social bargain' in the Republic of Ireland

Everyone pays taxes (apart from tax evaders): from the purchase of petrol to groceries to income and to social or national insurance we pay money to the state to provide certain services.

The system of taxation is hugely complex, with different groups competing in relation to how much should be paid and who should pay the most or the least. We frequently complain that we are taxed too much and receive a bad return on what we pay by way of health, housing, transport and other services. Yet, taxes provide essential social goods and services. The level and distribution of taxation is a matter of political choice and, ultimately, social values. The Republic of Ireland is not unusual in wanting to have European and even Scandinavian-level services but at US or UK level taxes.

By any measure, the Republic of Ireland is characterised by high levels of inequality in income before taxes and social welfare kick in, the same is true of the UK including Northern Ireland, representing a kind of 'bargain' whereby people pay less tax for fewer public services. Clearly the relationship between taxes and public spending is a complex one and is subject to variations in efficiency and effectiveness. However, it is broadly the case that we get what we pay for.

There is another aspect to the 'bargain' people experience in the Republic of Ireland: those on very low personal income tend to pay very little, if anything, by way of tax on income, but do of course pay a lot of taxes on goods and services – a point often overlooked in commentary on tax distribution. This represents an implicit social bargain. Lower-paid workers in hospitality, retail and other sectors receive less pay than their counterparts in similar European economies. However, the lower-paid in Ireland receive fewer public services. Households also pay taxes in the form of excise and VAT on consumer goods. Total taxes paid, including VAT and excise duty, are considerable. The taxation system extracts a fairly high proportion (between 20 and 30 per cent) of income (Collins, 2014). The strongly progressive nature of income taxes (especially because many low-income households pay little or no tax on their incomes) is offset by the strongly regressive nature of indirect taxes.

If the past is anything to go by, a hollowing out of the income tax base coupled with a downward movement in taxes on capital and corporate profits leaves the Republic of Ireland vulnerable to future shocks. Moreover, it is far from clear that the government has a clearly thought out strategy on how taxes should be reformed and at what level they should be pitched to pay for social goods and services such as health, education and affordable homes. There is a pro-cyclical tax-cutting dynamic, which has run according to a regular ten-year cycle since the 1970s:

- 1977: abolition of domestic rates and motor tax, coupled with a non-targeted 'Keynesian stimulus';
- 1987: a shrinking of social spending in key areas (notably local authority investment in social housing) and a reduction in taxes;
- 1997 onwards: promises of more tax cuts leading to slashing of capital gains tax from 40 to 20 per cent;
- 2007: promises of cuts to the top income tax rate;
- 2014: yet more promises to reduce or exempt people from income tax or the Universal Social Charge (USC).

Notwithstanding an increase in various income taxes relating to USC, PRSI and income tax following the crash of 2008, income taxes as a proportion of income paid in 2017 were much lower than they were in 1997 (Turnbull, 2018, p. 8).

The late Dr Garret FitzGerald asked a very pertinent question that is as relevant today as it was when written in the early months of 2008:

Why is it that, with a level of income higher than that of 22 of the 27 EU states, our public services fail to look after children in need or to care for the ill and the old; fail to make any serious attempt to rehabilitate our prisoners; and fail to ensure access to clean water – not to speak of failing to provide efficient competitive public transport, just to mention a few of our more obvious public service deficiencies? After all, over the past half century our political leaders were remarkably successful in securing much faster economic growth than anywhere else in Europe, moving Ireland from the poorest of the dozen countries in the northern part of Western Europe to becoming one of the richest. Given this success, why have our governments failed so miserably to deploy the vast resources thus created in such a way as to give us the kind of public services we can clearly afford and desperately need?[58]

How does the Republic of Ireland compare on taxation?

The Republic of Ireland and Northern Ireland are very much part of the story of a retrenchment in the role of the state. That this has happened is obscured by the fact that demands for public goods has increased in line with rising population and changing family structure. Rising incomes and expenditure across the whole economy has also made the declining share of public spending less obvious. Generally, the share of public spending has increased during periods of economic slowdown or recession and trended downwards during periods of recovery or growth in GDP.

A comparison of data provided by Eurostat and OECD does not support the view that general taxation, in the Republic of Ireland is high. Compared to the Northern European Comparator Group (NECG) the proportion of GDP is below average. Depending on which measure of total income (GDP or GNI) is used, the proportion of total income in the Republic of Ireland is in the region of 26.0 to 42.6 per cent in 2017. The NECG average on GDP was 46.5 per cent in 2017. The proportion varies sharply across EU states with the Baltic and some other Eastern European member states showing the lowest levels of taxation and the Scandinavian countries the highest. However, GDP provides a flawed measure due to distortions in some of its components. Goldrick-Kelly and McDonnell (2017) use the real value of government revenue per capita and point out that:

> In aggregate, we find that the Republic of Ireland raises significantly less in revenue (€8.1 billion) than it would if per capita taxes and social contributions were at the population weighted peer country average. The difference between the Republic of Ireland (€13,196) and the peer country weighted average (€14,953) in 2015 was €1,757 per person.

High-tax country or low-tax country? The question is not so easy to answer given the complexities around what constitutes total national income or output, especially in recent years. Taking total government tax revenue, a percentage of GDP or some statistically modified version of GNI may be misleading. Yet GDP remains the only basis on which compliance with fiscal debt and deficit rules are measured. Moreover, many seem to have difficulty in making up their minds about Irish GDP. If it is legitimate to claim that large portions of economic activity that are offshore are not relevant to real economic activity then it must be admitted that our position is not sustainable and not compatible with best international practice regarding investment and corporate taxes. If, on the other hand we treat such economic activity as being real and very much available as income to corporations, then we must use GDP in order to make comparisons. We cannot have it both ways. Working off some hybrid measure such as GNI*[59] is not intellectually coherent and is, in any case, based on a unique and possibly temporary Irish statistical solution to a very Irish statistical problem.

A widespread belief since the onset of the 2008 crash is that people are paying too much in taxation and need relief. Moreover, it is claimed unless a small, open economy such as Ireland cuts taxes it will lose out to competitor countries that can undercut on personal or corporate taxes. It is argued by some that by cutting taxes the government raises consumer confidence and encourages people to work harder or to supply more hours of work: this is known as the Laffer Curve effect in economics and is cited as a matter of faith by many politicians even though the empirical evidence is absent.

The 'war for talent' means that personal income tax is a consideration when skilled workers seek out employment in different countries. This is especially the case where, in English-speaking countries (to which Irish people have traditionally migrated), personal income taxes have been cut in recent decades. Were the Republic of Ireland to model itself on the UK or US and seek to emulate some Baltic EU member states we might find ourselves on a trajectory to ever-lower tax rates and, by direct consequences, a lower social wage. UK Chancellor of the Exchequer George Osborne captured this point succinctly in a speech to the UK Conservative Party conference in 2014 when he said,

> In a modern global economy where people can move their investment from one country to another at the touch of a button – and companies can relocate jobs overnight – the economics of high taxation are the economics of the past.[60]

Levels of personal taxation are much lower in English-speaking countries now than they were a generation ago. There is some validity in the claim that a small economy cannot diverge too much from international, European or English-speaking world norms. Since the trend is downward in many European countries – not least low-cost labour economies that are part of the new accession countries since 2004 – Ireland, North and South, needs to keep pace with these developments.

Taxes on employment fall under two headings: regular income tax and social insurance, known as Pay-Related Social Insurance (PRSI) in the Republic of Ireland and National Insurance Contributions in Northern Ireland and the rest of the UK. The balance between regular income tax and social insurance has changed dramatically during recent decades with proportionately more coming from income tax. Indeed, the UK and the Republic of Ireland have consistently been one of the lowest collectors of social insurance among EU member states.

An alternative approach to measuring comparative taxation rates is to focus on personal income tax rates. Starting with single persons, Figure 28 shows that those on the average wage in the Republic of Ireland pay the lowest amount in taxes (including PRSI, USC and 'ordinary' income tax) and contribute 19.4 per cent of their income on taxes. This figure does not include payment of VAT and excise duties, which as a percentage of income is higher for lower-income households and individuals: neither does it take into account the lower actual effective tax paid as a result of non-standard tax relief and exemptions – that is reliefs other than personal tax credits, PAYE tax credit or tax relief – for married or jointly assessed couples.

The Republic of Ireland leads the way as having the lowest average income tax rate for lower-paid single workers in 2017 (measured in this case as workers at 67 per cent of average earnings). At 12.5 per cent, the rate is very much below that of lower-paid workers in Germany where the estimate is 34.9 per cent. From the available data it is not possible to compare single persons on more than 167 per cent, of average earnings. With an average headline tax rate of 31.3 per cent, the Republic of Ireland comes eighteenth out of twenty-eight OECD countries for which data are available for 2017. Among the Northern EU comparator group, the Republic of Ireland has the second-lowest rate, just ahead of the UK.

The actual tax paid is somewhat less than this due to various reliefs (and it is very likely that such reliefs disproportionately benefit those on higher incomes because of pension, health and property tax reliefs). Even allowing for the distortion introduced by tax reliefs, other than the usual credits for singles or couples, the broad picture remains the same: for high-income earners the amount of income tax paid is not much above the average for other EU/OECD countries and well below what is paid by high-income individuals in Germany, the Netherlands, Belgium, Denmark and Sweden.

The case for personal income tax cuts in the Republic of Ireland often centres on the point at which single persons begin paying the higher rate of income tax. This is, relative to other countries, a low threshold. OECD data allow us to compare the headline marginal rate for different levels of income, just as is the case for average rates. Average-earning single persons paid a relatively high combined marginal income tax rate of 49 per cent, the fourth-highest among OECD countries. And where above-average income single earners are concerned (those at 167 per cent of average earnings), the marginal rate was eighth highest out of twenty-eight OECD countries. Ahead of the Republic of Ireland on that measure are Sweden, Belgium, Denmark, the Netherlands, Italy and Finland. Many of these countries manage to combine relatively high personal marginal tax rates with high-skill, high-productivity and dynamic economies.

Reforming our tax system

Taxation needs reform. This will take at least a decade if not decades. The following key principles are proposed:

- simplicity and transparency in the income tax code, including USC and PRSI;
- tax sufficiency in the aggregate to pay for an efficient and effective public service;

- a redistribution of tax liability so that higher-income and higher-wealth individuals pay more than they do currently and corporations pay an appropriate minimum effective rate of tax.

Public trust in government is vital to achieving the goal of public service reform and delivery. If people do not trust governments to tax fairly and to use tax revenues in ways that deliver the best outcomes in health, education, housing and so on then it is difficult to make the case for tax sufficiency to underpin universal public services. A root-and-branch reform of public service design, planning, governance and delivery is required. Similarly, reform of the tax code in a way that makes tax transparent and fair, levied in proportion to ability to pay, is the way to go. Taxpayers need to see the benefit of paying taxes and its impact on their communities through more explicit and transparent 'follow-the-money' channels.

A sensible approach to public finances is one governed by concern for the long-term risks and opportunities related to public assets and liabilities. If it makes sense to increase capital spending to boost capacity and head off risks in the medium-term or to put the brake on spending (or better still, raise taxes) when economies are growing rapidly and there is a risk of a domestic asset bubble then that is what governments should do. The experience of European politics and economics since the beginning of this millennium is that no amount of rules or laws can prevent foolish fiscal behaviour or address mismatches in banking and fiscal policy.

Everyone, especially those not in the top 10 per cent of the income and wealth distribution, pay a price for a poor social wage. Well-off people can opt out of limited public goods by buying their own private education, health and other services. But even high-income earners lose out in the long run because an unequal society fosters many social ills that impact on everyone, including the highest earners.

Carbon taxes

A shift in taxation from income to capital and from productive wealth to 'bads' such as carbon-intensive goods would significantly help in the international effort to combat climate change and environmental degradation. This could involve a gradual increase in carbon taxes over a fixed number of years. It would need to be done in such a way as to spread the charge between households and enterprises with the latter contributing a fixed sum as an additional part of corporate taxes. Revenue raised from carbon taxes should be ring-fenced for investment in renewable energy, retrofitting and public transport. Rather than implement carbon taxes from the top down or in isolation from other measures to give households currently reliant on car transport and home heating based on fossil fuels a choice, the Irish government should create a just transition fund that pays dividends to households ready to undergo retrofitting and transfer to alternative sources of energy including, for example, solar power.

On their own, carbon taxes will not save the planet but they can help modify patterns of human consumption and activity. Matching carbon taxes, supply-side measures should entail ambitious investment in renewables and energy-efficient homes, public buildings and enterprises. A redesign of social and income support programmes to avoid fuel poverty and other adverse impacts on households as a result of higher taxes on fuels is equally important.

Environmental taxes are required in helping to change citizen behaviour. By raising taxes on fossil fuels, governments can induce changes in usage and encourage household investment in better insulation and more efficient forms of heating. However, carbon taxes should not be paid for by cuts to income tax. On their own, carbon taxes are regressive, imposing a greater burden on poorer households in the absence of compensating social transfers or wage increases. Progressive income taxes have the advantage of redistributing income. It is necessary to offset increased carbon taxes with pro-equality measures such as wage increases weighted towards the lower paid and progressive taxes on income and wealth. While carbon taxes are explicit and visible, carbon subsidies tend to be implicit and invisible. A policy of investing in private car and road freight transport at the expense of public transport subsidises a heavier carbon footprint even if there is a gradual transition to lesser reliance on fossil fuels.

Social insurance

Social insurance needs to become what it says it is: a system of social insurance not unlike private health insurance or life assurance except that it is social in nature and covers the cost of public goods such as income protection, pensions, health and training. In principle everyone should pay regardless of income level on the grounds that they are paying into a common fund from which they draw benefit when needed. The notion that it is socially justifiable and fiscally sustainable for a large proportion of households and earners to be removed from the tax net (that is the income tax plus social insurance net) must be seriously challenged in public discourse. The answer to in-work poverty is a combination of a living wage and targeted social payments.

Income taxes

A way to avoid sharp cliffs in moving from a lower rate income tax rate (e.g., 20 per cent) to the higher rate (e.g., 40 per cent) is to revise income tax bands and rates to create a smoother transition from low to high incomes. This could be achieved through, for example, six tax rates stretching from 10 per cent up to 50 per cent. All tax credits and tax reliefs should be reviewed and eradicated except those that have a clear economic and social benefit and justification. Where new reliefs might be introduced they should be temporary and have a definite sunset clause.

Taxes on inheritance and gifts

These taxes badly require modernisation. Depending on the rate of taxation applied and the extent of exemptions granted to different categories of persons, there is scope for increasing the revenue yield. However, the main benefit of a reform to inheritance and gift taxes would not be increased revenue but the pursuit of the principle of equality. Ownership of wealth, especially housing, and the transfer of its value after death is a significant determinant of life chances for the coming generation. Were inheritance taxes to be made more effective in equalising total wealth and income, the benefits could accrue to the next generation but especially those less fortunate in the stakes of life where inheritance of property is concerned. One option to consider is the integration of inheritance tax into the current income tax system whereby income taxpayers are liable to pay tax on inheritance, which is counted as income in a given year. Thresholds could be applied below which no tax is paid. However, the progressivity of the income tax system could ensure that a progressive levy on very large amounts over a certain threshold is possible.

Current thresholds are much too high. In the absence of a comprehensive wealth tax other than the local property tax (which is a form of wealth tax, albeit on only one form of wealth such as people's homes) taxes on gifts and inheritance would provide a relatively efficient and non-economically disruptive method of redistributing wealth. The yield on capital acquisition tax is very modest – a fraction of one per cent of annual GDP. One option would be to increase such a tax and to link the proceeds to a People's Fund, as discussed earlier.

Taxes on the stock of wealth

The idea of a wealth tax has been discussed at different times: efforts to introduce a wealth tax in the Republic of Ireland in the 1970s were met with stiff opposition at the time and the tax introduced in 1975 was short-lived.

Personal wealth broadly encompasses housing, land, financial assets and other valuable goods. Combining the value of these components and deducting the value of debts gives personal net wealth. This amount, estimated in a survey of the Central Bank–Central Statistics Office in 2015, varies across households. Reflecting high levels of owner-occupied dwellings, much wealth is concentrated in households that live in properties whose value has appreciated sharply in recent decades and on which there is little or no offsetting debt. Older people are often owners of such properties as the data provided by the CSO indicate.

There is a case for a net wealth tax which would combine all forms of wealth including housing. Currently, there are only two forms of taxation on wealth: capital acquisition tax, which is a levy on the transfer of capital usually when someone dies (a one-off tax applied to a lump sum) and local property tax (LPT) introduced in 2011 and based on frozen property values at 2013 values.

The proceeds of LPT were intended for use in financing local public services. In practice, the link between LPT and local public services is far from obvious although local authorities do have limited discretion to vary the rate of LPT. Objections to the LPT include concerns about household ability to pay. Existing thresholds are low, meaning that households on medium incomes (in the €25,000 to €35,000 income range) are liable to pay a few hundred euro a year depending on the notional value of their property. No account is taken of the extent of outstanding mortgage debts. There is a case to review current arrangements and to develop a local-based net wealth tax based on the combined net wealth of households but with thresholds of liability adjusted to reflect specific circumstances. McDonnell (2013) has discussed options for a wealth tax in the Republic of Ireland in some detail.

Corporation taxes

Taxation on the income or profits of corporations is a highly contested area. The average effective rate of tax on corporations has fallen sharply across the advanced economies over the last half century. The Republic of Ireland has been to the fore in reducing corporation tax as a tool for attracting and retaining foreign direct investment. This has not been without some controversy including at European level where some of the larger member states together with the European Commission would prefer to harmonise and consolidate corporate tax at the EU level. The rising complexity of cross-border investment and trade along with tax-minimising corporate strategies making use of differences in national and international tax law has enabled some well-known corporations to pay extremely low rates of tax. The overall average rate of corporation tax is probably somewhere in the region of 10 per cent of taxable profits in the Republic of Ireland. However, this is an average across trading corporations and the basis of calculation (taxable profits) is subject to estimation.

While a precise comparison of effective corporate tax rate across countries is challenging, it is clear that average effective rates are significantly lower in Ireland than most other advanced economies. Low corporate tax rates are, after all, one of the main selling points of successive Irish governments in attracting investors. Every trading corporation, including domestic enterprises, benefits from such low rates of tax.

Profit shifting is a significant feature of multinational activity in Ireland making it difficult to identify and estimate the true level of economic activity on which corporate tax is paid. It is clear, however, that at a global level, societies are very much shortchanged as a result of these activities and the international race to reduce corporation tax rates. In the long run a move to undercut competitors is self-defeating as nearly every country joins in the process. International solidarity and cooperation could stop this trend and ensure that corporations pay some minimum effective level of tax. In the case of Ireland it would not be unreasonable to expect all corporations to pay a minimum effective rate of tax, which would still be well below the nominal 'headline' rate but higher than say 5 per cent.

8

New Enterprises

We ignore, at our peril, the role of enterprises in creating wealth and living standards, including the social wage. We should see enterprises more as social institutions where human labour (or human capital) works with knowledge, or tools or other materials to create goods and services of value to people. A new and more diversified set of enterprise models is required, placing human labour and human flourishing at the centre of enterprises culture.

This chapter outlines ideas for taking enterprise forward and realising new models of enterprise performance. It challenges some of the traditional assumptions and focusses on the role of enterprises as a key lever to bring about long-term social and economic change. Environmental change provides a huge opportunity for small and medium-sized enterprises to target new markets and activities, including services and products that will enable Ireland to transition to a low- and eventually a zero-carbon economy.

I have paid much attention so far to the role of the State in providing public services and driving an improvement in working conditions and pay but the central importance of enterprise in social and economic life is easily overlooked. In fact there has been a marked tendency to relegate notions of competitiveness, productivity and entrepreneurship to the realm of an employer- or business-led discourse only.

To the extent that trade unions or progressive political forces have embraced a discussion of the role of the enterprise, it has taken one of two forms: calls for the state to own or better regulate business activity or efforts to improve the conditions and rights of labour within existing enterprises. Enterprise development or industrial strategy must include the role of the state as a driver and a facilitator of growth in enterprises and productivity. However, this is only one part to the problems of low productivity and imbalanced market structure identified in Chapter 2. Less attention has been paid to the possibility of new forms of wealth or social value creation and corresponding forms of enterprise owned and operated according to different principles and structures normally in vogue. The notion of a third force emerging to lead on the development of new market-changing enterprises is rarely considered. An example of this is the lack of attention to the role of new forms of social credit in direct competition with large private banks or formally owned public banks operated according to private sector norms.

We need to think in terms of developing new exporting enterprises based on strong indigenous small and medium-sized enterprises and some large ones competing on global markets where Ireland could further develop its competitive advantage in key product and service areas. These could include natural resources of wind, grass and water, agribusiness, English language education, pharma, new economy ICT services, health services and construction services.

The weak link in the chain: domestic enterprise in the Republic of Ireland

Small and medium-sized enterprises, defined as enterprises with fewer than 250 employees, are the backbone of the economy in both parts of the island of Ireland. The most recent demographic business data released by the CSO confirm that SMEs in the Republic of Ireland accounted for over 99.8 per cent of all businesses in 2015, contributed almost one half of all GVA in the state and provided employment for over two in three persons employed in the business economy.[61] Business SMEs account for the bulk of net additional employment in the non-agricultural sector since mid 2012.

As noted in Chapter 2, a mixed picture emerges from a collection of indicators relevant to enterprise performance including levels of management capacity, investment in innovation and scale of intellectual property. Patenting activity is well below comparative OECD and EU averages for similar type sectors. A number of recent OECD economic surveys of Ireland highlight the relative weakness of Irish-owned enterprises in terms of productivity and integration in what they termed 'global value chains' where enterprise re-export imported inputs.[62] Technological innovation is less developed among such enterprises than is the case in other countries. Barriers to greater research and development activity by enterprises relate to the cost of, and availability of, research and development resources as well as access to finance and lack of developed higher education-enterprise links. This is the case even though total labour costs are generally lower here than in most other advanced EU economies.

The huge expansion in services since the 1990s has transformed the landscape of the economies and workforce of Ireland. Manufacturing has seen a major downturn in traditional areas not least because of global competition and technological change. Because of industrialisation, agriculture has greatly diminished. New areas of manufacturing have prospered especially in agri-food where exporters have been highly successful. The pharmaceutical sector accounted for over half of all goods exports in the Republic of Ireland in 2014. The nature of production has become much more complex, involving multiple sources of inputs across global chains. In the domain of information technology and business services, physical location for any given activity may be difficult to identify as intellectual property is traded in an increasingly borderless world.

The domestic enterprise model includes low value-added, low-wage sectors with just over 40 per cent of the indigenous workforce in the non-financial market economy employed in the distributive and hospitality sectors, well above Northern European norms. This has also been accompanied by a long-standing reliance on housing and property with an aversion to high value-added activities. Manufacturing has been relatively minor compared to other mainland European economies. There are some impressive exceptions but this is the overall conclusion. A particular failure of native enterprise noted in many previous studies including that of O'Hearn (2001) has been the lack of a sufficiently strong local market for products and services that could serve as centres of innovation and expansion.

Innovation drives growth in enterprise output. Jacobson (2013, p. 47) defines innovation as 'A new or significantly improved product (good or service) introduced to the market or the introduction within an enterprise of a new or significantly improved process.'

Another indicator of innovation activity is use of venture capital funding by enterprises where Irish companies perform well below EU averages. While care is needed in cross-country statistical comparisons it appears that total innovation activity as a percentage of company turnover is below average in the Republic of Ireland. However, the estimated proportion of GDP spent by enterprises on innovation activities is relatively high in the Republic of Ireland (CSO, 2018c). Moreover, above-average rates of innovation activity in Irish enterprises were identified in the EU Community Innovation Survey in the period 2008–10.

Gross expenditure on research and development (GERD) is close to European averages but is well below that of the Nordic countries. GERD includes business, government and higher-education funding. Not surprisingly, a large amount of GERD effort, in the case of the Republic of Ireland, is concentrated in foreign-owned firms. Private business funding of research and development in the higher education sector is lower in the Republic of Ireland than in other Northern European countries.

Data published by the CSO in 2018 shows that foreign-owned enterprises accounted for 64 per cent (or €2.9 billion) of all innovation-related expenditure in 2016. Of this, €1.4 billion was for in-house research and development. Almost 36 per cent of Irish-owned enterprises reported innovation-related expenditure in the reference period compared to 43 per cent of foreign-owned enterprises. Innovation is strongly related to enterprise size as one in three small enterprises (10–49 employees) reported spending on innovation, while two out of three large enterprises (250 employees plus) had such expenditure in 2016. In a recent publication of the 2017 EU Industrial Research and Development Investment Scoreboard, twenty-three companies based in Ireland were included in the global research and development ranking of 2,500 companies.

Many (though by no means all) domestic enterprises have lacked critical size, incentive or support to invest in upskilling, research, innovation and exporting. In 2011 (before the surge in corporate activity and associated statistical distortions in 2015), the top fifty enterprises in the Republic of Ireland accounted for 35 per cent of total turnover; 41 per cent of total GVA; and 61 per cent of total gross operating surplus (Dalton, 2014).

The OECD in its most recent Economic Survey of Ireland in 2018 pointed out that 'the capacity of local firms to absorb and implement new technologies is impeded by relatively weak managerial skills. This partly reflects the low proportion of workers participating in lifelong learning activities.' Productivity in Irish-owned enterprises has been largely stagnant over the 2006–16 decade. By contrast, foreign-owned firms have surged ahead, influenced in part by reclassification of activities from 2015 (Figure 30).

OECD comparisons of productivity indicate that many economies are characterised by a minority of high-productivity 'frontier firms' that invest more than other firms in research and development. This tends to lead to innovation. The degree of diffusion of innovation from frontier to non-frontier firms varies over time and across jurisdictions. It is likely that the extent of diffusion has slowed down in some of the major OECD economies (OECD, 2015). The observed slowdown in measured productivity in the last fifteen years in most of the major economies appears to be linked to a slowdown in the rate of innovation diffusion as distinct from the rate of innovation in the frontier enterprises. Mobility of labour as well as the integration and networking of enterprises help diffuse knowledge and innovation within and across national boundaries. The slowdown may also be due to some workers being under-qualified or over-qualified for their jobs. Additionally, small start-up enterprises need careful nurturing and support with a more proactive role for existing business networks, higher education and public agencies.

A similar story in Northern Ireland

The immediate challenges are not dissimilar to those facing the indigenous sector in the Republic of Ireland in terms of under-employment, lack of sufficient investment and innovation alongside inadequate levels of skill and organisational capacity. A strategy to boost investment and generate new and better-quality jobs must involve a range of policies and not rely on one particular domain, such as attracting foreign inward investment. SMEs will continue to provide the bulk of employment in Northern Ireland. However, there is a need to develop particular areas of enterprise in this sector with appropriate public sector support and funding. Rather than identifying market winners, the role of public sector support could be focussed initially on providing a significant boost to basic research (Mac Flynn, 2016).

While Northern Ireland continues to lag behind other UK regions, levels of unemployment, under-employment, poverty, personal indebtedness and exclusion from the labour market point to a need for a politically realistic strategy to rebuild Northern Ireland's economy and society around a different vision that can be shared by all communities. This will be made even more difficult following Brexit.

A debate centred on rebalancing the economy away from the public to the private sector misses the point that a combined and mutually reinforcing strategy to develop both parts of the economy is required, including voluntary or not-for-profit sectors that provide important goods and services. It does not necessarily follow that the public sector, by stepping out of its former or current roles, opens up a space for more private-sector activity. A strategic role for government and various public agencies could release valuable local skills and resources as well as attract partnerships with companies and agencies in other parts of the world. By contrast, a vision focussed on a low-wage and 'flexible' labour market model (where hiring, firing and contractual arrangements are mainly to the advantage of employers) would leave Northern Ireland vulnerable to external shifts and shocks and do little to foster an egalitarian, participative society.

A major challenge for enterprises in Northern Ireland is a continuing deficiency in leadership and management skills, which are below the level of comparable companies in other developed economies. Data published in *Management Matters in Northern Ireland and the Republic of Ireland* (Department of Enterprise, Trade and Investment, 2009) indicate that 'over half (52 per cent) of the gap with the US is due to structural factors such as firm size, ownership and skill levels'. Productivity as measured by gross value added per person employed is relatively low in sectors such as business services, finance and ICT. Northern Ireland remains much less export-oriented than the Republic of Ireland. In terms of input and investment, total spending on R&D remains very low in Northern Ireland. Externally-owned enterprises account for 75 per cent of R&D investment. Some 40 per cent of workers in the non-financial business economy in Northern Ireland are employed in wholesale, retail, food and tourist accommodation. The corresponding figure for the EU15 domestic economies is 34 per cent (Goldrick-Kelly and Mac Flynn, 2018).

The decline of manufacturing in both parts of the island of Ireland reflects global trends. The relatively large growth in service may be flattered to the extent that the real price of many manufactured goods has fallen (e.g., the relative price of computers, mobile phones and other goods) and many in-firm services are now outsourced to specialist service companies whose activity was previously recorded under manufacturing.

The notion that manufacturing reflects an earlier stage of economic development and is to be associated with low-grade, low-wage and low-skill activities is incorrect. Many manufacturing firms, such as Wrightbus and Bombardier, are engaged in high-value-added activities employing high-skill workers and driving research and innovation such. Manufacturing holds the key to developing new forms of energy extraction and carbon-reducing technologies with applications across the whole island's economy.

Maintenance of a low corporation tax, or its further possible reduction in the case of Northern Ireland, does not constitute a sustainable or globally ethical strategy to promote economic development in the medium term. The administrative complexities involved in implementing a special low rate for Northern Ireland would impose burdens on companies and public agencies. There is no compelling evidence that such a tax cut for corporations will stimulate inward investment on a scale required to transform industry and services in Northern Ireland. Paradoxically, possible additional restrictions on public spending in areas such as education and training, roads and other areas of social and environmental infrastructure would harm the Northern Ireland economy even more.

The industrial strategy consultation document published in Northern Ireland in early 2017 (Department for the Economy, 2017) identified five pillars for economic growth: acceleration of innovation and research; improvements to education, skills and employability; driving inclusive and sustainable growth; succeeding in global markets; and building the best economic infrastructure. Inward foreign direct investment is an important source of growth, but good enterprise policy requires a more diversified approach. There is potential for a state-led approach to industrial planning, which would seek to identify new opportunities that enhance export potential and ability to compete in the domestic market.

A report by InterTradeIreland (2015) identified opportunities for cross-border coordination among establishments of higher education, public agency and businesses in medical devices and health information. Northern Ireland has a vibrant, locally-owned medical devices sector with potential for development and a number of successful market niches in aerospace, pharmaceuticals and space technology as well as in the small but growing cyber security sector.

Some ongoing challenges in Northern Ireland include elevated costs associated with energy, transport and distribution as well as legacy effects of under-investment in many areas of economic infrastructure, not least telecommunication networks in rural areas.

Business expenditure on research and development (BERD) remains low in local and small enterprises. One area where Northern Ireland does comparatively well in UK terms is in the number of spin-off companies from higher education institutions where the rate has been in excess of that across the UK. Public agencies such as Invest Northern Ireland have been successful in helping thousands of enterprises to take off, from aerospace to ICT, to renewable energy.

The reasons for a relatively weak domestic enterprise sector in Northern Ireland are complex (as they are in the Republic of Ireland). The decline in traditional manufacturing, textile, shipbuilding and associated engineering firms in the post-war period was never offset by adequate growth in other enterprises. A combination of demographic and political factors resulted in a relative increase in the size of public administration. Long-term constraints and under-supply of export or enterprise expertise were exacerbated by the credit crunch facing many SMEs during the recent recessionary period. While there have been outstanding successes, a stronger enterprise sector is still needed to lift Northern Ireland's economy.

Actions for a dynamic domestic enterprise economy

A major challenge in realising a long-term vision for Ireland will be the development of a stronger, internationally resilient business sector as well as a strategy to develop local but export-oriented small and medium-sized enterprises.

Building on success and focusing on new initiatives and sectors

Future prospects for the development of indigenous enterprises on both sides of the border could encompass sectors such as agri-food, energy renewables, education services, cloud computing and construction (with the possibility of marketing retrofitting and skills and capacity). Areas that will require particular attention include supply chains, skills of employees and managers, organisational capacity, marketing, design and innovation. Examples of sectors where new enterprises could flourish include:

- highly differentiated and branded dairy products aimed at expanding markets in Asia and South America;
- construction-related activities focussed on insulation and high-quality craft with energy-saving benefits in both parts of the island of Ireland and the potential for export;
- locally-based energy cooperatives where communities invest and pool resources to avail of wind and solar energy;
- education and training services aimed at emerging markets including English language training and cultural studies;
- tourism initiatives where better management and international marketing of green cycleways, walking routes and other amenities could prove highly effective, building on the success of initiatives such as the Wild Atlantic Way;
- information technology start-ups focussed on market niches, taking advantage of Ireland's relatively easy access to EU and US markets.

The uncertainty of Brexit has created an urgent, all-island challenge to develop skills, re-skill and prepare. The creation of a wholesale single electricity market (SEM) in 2007 was of huge importance and should be defended at all costs, notwithstanding UK withdrawal from the EU. The SEM which, since October 2018, has developed into the integrated single electricity market (ISEM), stems from a bilateral UK-Republic of Ireland agreement. Maintaining a data privacy framework to enable the ISEM to continue is vital. This could be achieved by continued compliance with EU regulations possible under a 'Norwegian' or European Economic Area arrangement; in this case both parts of Ireland would remain in a Single European Market with common standards and rules governing trade and movement of goods and services.

The biggest immediate threat to all-island trade is uncertainty about Brexit. This uncertainty extends not only to physical customs inspection associated with goods but to the hundreds of regulations and standards associated with particular products and services inside and outside the single European market. These divergences will require some level of monitoring in relation to trade in goods and services in all directions across the EU–UK frontiers.

Widening ownership of enterprises

Labour should be seen as a key factor in production and value added rather than simply a production cost, with enterprises belonging to a social space with multiple stakeholders involved. Workplace representation and collective bargaining coverage need to be strengthened. New forms of partnership and participation could enhance company performance and productivity.

Recent decades have seen a marked shift in ownership of capital from public to private domains. Privatisation or partial privatisation of key utilities, telecommunications, energy, transport and particular services such as waste collection and disposal has been accepted by most political parties under the pretext of offering better services or choice to consumers. The results are unfolding gradually as the fruits of competition are manifest in many cases of under-investment, inefficient duplication of providers and withdrawal or non-supply of important goods and services to particular localities or population groups. Now is the time to widen ownership of the economy by encouraging a greater diversity of ownership types embracing state, local governmental, semi-state commercial, workers' and producers' cooperatives, public equity holding in private start-up ventures as well as privately owned firms.

A new, democratically-managed enterprise could have some or all of the following characteristics and be:

- owned and managed by a range of interests including workers, members and organisations of the community;
- run for a shared community goal and economic interest rather than profit;
- focussed on serving local markets and sourcing local or regional materials in the first instance while developing national or global markets on a solid local foundation;
- run according to criteria of equality or treatment, sustainability of resource utilisation and re-use of material as well as democratic participation in shared decision-making.

Although written over thirty years ago, the following extract from an ESRI publication (Kennedy and Healy, 1985, p. 83) still has relevance in considering a strategy to develop locally-based but export-oriented small and medium-sized enterprises:

> In making these points, however, we would not claim that the encouragement of new small enterprises in the private sector is the only, or perhaps even the main, avenue to the development of indigenous manufacturing entrepreneurship. The development of established private enterprise, the scope for new forms of enterprise such as

workers' or producers' cooperative, and even the possibility of direct state manufacturing enterprise in selected areas, are also major areas that should be considered.

Different types of enterprises across the globe coexist and compete with other enterprises for the benefit of local communities. These might take the form of workers' cooperatives, municipal enterprises and civil society and social enterprises run on a not-for-profit basis. The possibility of new enterprises being established by local authorities or as part of existing commercial state enterprises is worth exploring.

Denmark is an example of how worker-run or community-run cooperatives have flourished in recent decades in response to the oil crisis of the early 1980s. Such is the success of new enterprises founded on community ownership and generation of electricity from wind turbines that Denmark has captured a big share of world output of wind turbines. Many jobs have been created in renewable energy activities.

A model based on localised but coordinated and well-integrated energy policies helped transform Denmark's dependency on imported oil and gas. This model was based on public investment concentrated on new wind turbines over a prolonged period from the 1980s, the introduction of an *Energipakken* obliging electricity distribution companies to purchase a certain quota of supply every year from renewable producers and the encouragement of local and community-owned wind turbines using 'residency criteria' to ensure local ownership.[63]

While the Danish success is associated with specific cultural and institutional characteristics it is not beyond the imagination and capacity of state agencies working in cooperation with local communities to generate alternative business models in areas where jobs are under immediate threat as is the case in coal and peat-burning electricity generating stations in parts of Ireland.

Workplace democracy and employee participation in decision-making, which has some currency in Germany and the

Scandinavian countries, should be part of a strategy to renew enterprises, raise productivity and improve social outcomes. Company legislation should be changed in relation to medium and larger enterprises to strengthen the voice of a range of actors, including employees and the wider community.

A paper by Nolan, Perrin and Gorman (2013) shows the potential for a small but strongly connected workers' cooperative movement in Northern Ireland. The idea of worker cooperatives is not a remote and marginal idea but one that could be taken up and applied in specific cases of company closure, unmet local needs or innovative social entrepreneurship. Across the UK there are an estimated 400 worker cooperatives with 2,000 members and 2,000 employees, yet there are scarcely any on the island of Ireland. Worker cooperatives are more common in a number of European countries such as Spain and Italy.

The legal infrastructure to facilitate and protect, where appropriate, existing and new worker cooperatives needs attention. Some of the reasons for past failures or lack of current interest or tradition with regard to the establishment of worker cooperatives are to do with a range of factors, including a lack of appropriate legal, accounting and marketing expertise, a lack of interest from relevant public or civil society agencies and no appropriate support and protection for individuals and communities taking an initial risk.

The Industrial and Provident Societies (Amendment) Bill 2018 should be considered as an important contribution to implementing reform in this area.

Reforming company culture

Haldane (2016) considers the options for public policy to lean against short-termism in the way that some companies are run. To counter behaviour that maximises short-term gain for executives or shareholders, a number of measures could be used such as remuneration packages which incentivise long-term gains as well as changes to corporate governance that increase the influence and voting power of long-term shareholders, as is the practice in France. An example of incentives for CEOs is to ensure that at least one half of bonuses are in the form of debt or equity, implying that a payback only occurs on the basis of positive and results-yielding performance.

'Companies of excellence' could operate on the basis of co-determination or co-responsibility involving workers, managers and other stakeholders. By adopting principles of ethical business behaviour, compliance with sectoral sustainable goals and limitation of pay differentials within enterprises, these companies of excellence could be rewarded with distinctions and their brand image promoted on domestic and overseas markets. Additionally, in large companies a voice for workers should be present on boards of management as well as remuneration committees where such exist.

Creating a more supportive environment

Words such as 'pro-enterprise', 'business-friendly' and 'social risk' are often used as the opposite of 'security', 'state planning' and 'egalitarianism'. In reality there is no reason to think or speak as if one set of ideas is incompatible with the other. Security can be a springboard for risk-taking and innovation, for example, when start-up entrepreneurs benefit from a social protection net in case of business failure. An active state boosts private-sector productivity, investment and innovation. Egalitarian incomes and public service policy can sit readily with an economically efficient country.

We need to cultivate an environment that supports SMEs. Costs, including tax rates and breaks, have their role but the evidence does not point towards Ireland being a high-cost location compared to other Northern European economies. A dynamic enterprise culture can coexist with an active, dynamic state.

Regulation is not necessarily inimical to innovation or the creation of a culture of entrepreneurship.

Thinking about industrial policy and strategy has evolved in recent decades. Rather than undertaking centralised and targeted interventions in areas such as science, innovation and technology, many writers emphasise the role of general purpose technologies and the infrastructural requirements for a modern economy and society as well as the need for long-term strategic support. The role of the state, in this context, could be that of enabler as well as investor in the supporting infrastructure of broadband, information networks and financial backing.

The concept of an 'entrepreneurial state' championed by Jacobs and Mazzucato (2016, p. 99) and others is compatible with the fostering of a dynamic, entrepreneurial society. The industrial strategy consultation document published in Northern Ireland (Department for the Economy, 2017, p. 9) refers to 'an economy where entrepreneurship and enterprise is endemic and reflected in a growing status as a start-up region' while calling for 'a more entrepreneurial public sector'.

The role of government is currently seen, at best, as a champion and facilitator rather than a joint actor and partner. If its role is confined to setting the regulatory and institutional context and ensuring a level playing field, then we miss a crucial aspect of economic development as experienced over the decades. In other words, the role of the state is not just as a fixer of market failure but as an actor in shaping and creating markets.

Ó Riain (2004) argues that the Irish State played an essential role in developing the economy in the 1990s, especially with regard to the high-tech industry. This involved the fostering of local learning and innovation networks helped by the use of decentralised state institutions, which draw on local, national and global networks and relationships. Research by Jenkins et al. (2008) based on long-term case studies in the US suggests that grant and loan programmes for new technology, along with technology research parks, have positive impacts on regional growth while controlling for location and agglomeration factors.

An active and enabling state supporting domestic enterprise could include:

- Expanded commercial activity of existing public enterprise companies in key areas such as broadband, water, social housing, transport and renewable energy with a target of keeping public investment, including exchequer and off-the-books investment equivalent, at a level of 5 per cent of national income.
- The development of new municipal enterprises equipped to deliver services and products, including social housing in local authority areas. These enterprises could work with private enterprises and borrow from a state investment bank.
- The channelling of early-stage venture capital to companies through a state investment bank.
- A new model of apprenticeship training expanded to include new skills and occupations and with a target for company investment of 3 per cent of total labour costs funded from an expanded model of social insurance.
- A reappraisal of active labour market policies to incorporate aspects of a Nordic 'flexi-secure' pathway for retraining, income protection and work guarantee in exchange for mobility of labour across firms and sectors.
- An increase in total research and development spending by government, business and other entities to 3 per cent of national income by 2021.

An all-island development bank would be an important part of adapting to Brexit: with the investment support of the UK and Irish governments along with the European Investment Bank. Such a development bank could help SMEs with advice, training, loans and equity holdings.

The government plays a key role in the development of innovation inputs, most importantly through its funding of R&D, education and knowledge infrastructure. The Irish government's Innovation 2020 strategy commits to a research intensity target of 2 per cent of GDP with one quarter of this coming from public investment in R&D. Tom McDonnell (2017) makes the case that public spending on research and development and higher education needs to be stepped up. This can particularly benefit SMEs who may face funding, talent and marketing constraints. Figure 31 demonstrates the weakness of public spending on R&D among comparable European countries similar to Ireland either by virtue of size or overall level of economic development.

Innovative capacity depends on more than just R&D. It is also a function of education and skills levels, the cost of acquiring knowledge, supportive government policies and the quality of capital markets among other things. Mariana Mazzucato points out that Germany's successful competitiveness strategy is driven by its ability to build a strong innovation system, with patient long-term finance (through, for example, the KfW Development Bank), strong science-industry links (Fraunhofer institutes) and above-average R&D/GDP spending.

Democratising credit

The scale and impact of the banking collapse in 2008 points towards fundamental and serious ownership, governance and regulatory flaws in the years leading up to 2008. Crucial to enterprise development is banking and its interaction with investment, savings and lending policies. Even with a significant economic recovery in both jurisdictions since 2014, many small and medium-sized businesses still find it challenging to access credit. With a significant amount of outstanding non-performing loans in the system there is a risk that access and choice for savers and borrowers will continue to be restricted. The prospects of foreign-owned banking should be a matter of concern given the strategic importance of banking not only at national level but in local and rural economies.

The establishment of a state investment bank would be an important help in channelling investment into SMEs which face difficulties in accessing affordable finance. Lending could be complemented by the use of advisory and early warning facilities to strengthen companies and raise standards of efficiency and performance. Such a bank would be well placed to pool risk and assist innovation start-ups. A reformed banking system is central to a stronger social and local enterprise dimension – something that was largely lost in the lead-up to 2008 when Irish banks behaved irresponsibly in relation to the scale and composition of lending. Lessons can be learned from the experience of banking in the 1930s when the Irish state set up the Industrial Credit Company as well as the experience of public development banks in other countries (notably in Germany where the KfW has been highly successful since the 1950s). Vic Duggan (2013) has outlined the options for establishing such a body.

A state retail bank allied to a state investment bank could provide a focus for enhanced competition and choice for savings and oversight of lending. The high degree of concentration and lack of competition in the Irish banking system is troubling. A third force banking network could change the sector by shifting part of market power to a more decentralised and locally-based network of banks or credit unions offering a range of services and run according to a different set of business principles to those which prevailed in the run-up to the Irish banking collapse of 2008.

Banking and credit is a vital nerve centre of economic activity. There is a compelling case for retaining public ownership of some areas of banking and credit rather than ceding the entire sector back to the private sector. The crash of 2008 illustrated not only the need for more effective public regulation of banks and credit unions but the urgency for institutions to be held in public ownership and run in a democratic fashion to the benefit of many savers and borrowers. A case for a return to 'plain banking' and a clearer separation of risky investment and lending from retail local banking services is compelling. A vibrant and significant network of local banks and credit unions prior to 2007 could have mitigated the impact of the Irish banking collapse.

The present duopoly arrangement in the Republic of Ireland where two large commercial banks operate a monoculture based on shareholder principles and a cost-reducing and profit-maximising imperative as evidenced by the scandals associated with tracker mortgages in 2017 needs to be challenged. There is scope for a third banking force, held in public or cooperative ownership and offering choice, competition and alternative sources of credit for businesses and households.

The credit union movement could also be developed. Credit unions are owned by over 2 million people in the Republic of Ireland but are very restricted in their range of credit activities. They are confined to lending on the basis of members' savings, with surplus savings largely held on deposits with the commercial banks at extremely low interest rates.

Models of good practice exist in other countries. For example, the *Sparkasse* network of public savings banks number 400 independent, locally-owned banks in Germany. They provide important lines of credit to households and businesses (including, for example, the much acclaimed *mittelstand* enterprises that drive a significant share of German export success). The *Sparkasse* banks are owned in perpetuity by the whole community under German public law. They cannot be bought or sold. A vital component of the success of these banks are the central service providers. Comparative research into the performance of community banks by Kurt Mettenheim and Olivier Butzbach (2015) indicates positive outcomes for such banks, including cases of competitive advantages over the mainstream banks. Locally-based banks operating according to a good legal and ethical framework can outperform at low risk on costs as well as responsiveness.

A revamped credit union network could engage in commercial lending to facilitate house-building and access to credit by prospective homeowners. However, systems of governance and oversight would need to be strengthened. Such local banks could work in partnership with local authorities, business interests and voluntary groups as well as the proposed HCI.

In association with An Post and other bodies it should be possible to develop a new national savings bank for small to medium-sized savers and business borrowers alongside a new national investment bank focussed on long-term strategic investment, including the development of infrastructure and renewable energy sources. Such a service could offer a locally-based, full range of retail banking services including debit cards, cash withdrawal by ATM and lending.

Managing water and waste

A large programme of investment is required for Ireland's age-ing water infrastructure. Significant loss of water is a symptom of a system that has suffered from under-investment. Water user charges are supposed to encourages efficiency and create a revenue stream to fund a commercial enterprise (such as Irish Water) at a sufficient level to enable it to undertake the nec-essary investments over the next decades. On the other hand, the argument for 'free water' is that a genuinely progressive tax system (whether local or national) will guard against 'water poverty' and ensure that people pay for water in proportion to their means as distinct from their usage. Resistance to 'com-modification' of the water sector impedes developments in the direction of privatisation.

Water is becoming the new oil (Ogle, 2016, p. 26). McDonnell (2014) sets out a more equitable reckoning of water-charging were waste charges to be re-introduced for households. The risk in taking the road of water commodification for all households (and not just for those in private group schemes) is that it opens the door to privatisation through EU competition rules, EU fiscal rules or changes in domestic political circumstances. The supply of fresh water will increasingly become a central bad break for governments, investors and communities. In many parts of the world access to drinking water is severely restricted due to environmental factors as well as large-scale under-investment in the necessary infrastructure. A regime of water-charging may, in some cases, tip households into extreme poverty.

How to manage and deliver water, as well as collect and dispose of waste, is certainly a controversial subject. A process of 'commodification' of water typically precedes privatisation. The pattern of privatisation of water and waste is well established. However, examples stand out of publicly owned water services and even, in some cases, re-nationalisation or re-municipalisation of water services.

Harnessing our natural resources

There is a strange parallel between the mistaken notion of Ireland's mid-twentieth century lack of natural resources and the huge untapped offshore wind energy resources. It is the reverse side of a natural resource bonanza like the one that occurred in Norway.[64,65]

Opportunities exist for SMEs to become more involved in recycling activities at different stages in product and material lifecycles. Even if some sectors, such as food, will be tested to the limits of enterprise endurance by whatever outcome Brexit yields in the medium term, there is a need now for agencies such as Enterprise Ireland to ramp up its intelligence, coaching and advisory role in helping companies to identify new opportunities. The circular economy is one such opportunity, not least when it involves eco-design for longer-lasting products as well as restorative production processes.

The challenges raised by Brexit together with the long-term goal of achieving a zero-carbon economy means that a circular economy needs to become not just a talking point but a rally to action by households, enterprises, governments and trade unions. The 2017 IMPACT/FÓRSA publication, *A Just Transition to a Low-Carbon Economy Implications for IMPACT and Its Members*, provides a very timely and useful contribution to a much-needed debate in the trade union movement, as does the SIPTU report, *There Are No Jobs on a Dead Planet: What a Just Transition Means for Workers*. Both of these reports acknowledge the harm being caused by climate change and the need for urgent action to redirect productive activities and retrain and upskill workers in currently high-carbon-based sectors.

The island of Ireland is rich in natural resources, ranging from discovered and undiscovered deposits of natural gas off the coastline to ocean and wind power, biomass and solar energy. The current special rates of corporation tax, including the profit resource rent tax (PRRT) should be raised. The Fossil Fuel Divestment Bill (2016) has shown the way, however, in diverting public investment away from fossil-fuel sectors.

The technology associated with renewable energy sources is constantly evolving, making it ever more economical and attractive. The ESB is charting its own way forward. It plots a course towards decarbonisation in the production of electricity and plans that, in the near future, over 40 per cent of electricity will be generated from renewable sources (primarily hydro and wind) compared to 27 per cent in 2015. Just under 20 per cent of total greenhouse emissions were from electricity-generating power stations).

There is concern, even in the very short run, about the future of the coal-burning Moneypoint electricity generation plant in County Clare as well as the peat-burning stations in the midlands. A just transition to sustainable electricity generation based on strategies involving training, diversification and growth in new forms of enterprise must come to the fore. A shift away from fossil fuel (in particular oil and gas, both of which are heavily imported via Great Britain) in the provision of energy in the various sectors will require major adjustments in infrastructure and application of new technologies.

Agriculture, transport and home heating make up the bulk of contribution to greenhouse gas (GHG) emissions but the electricity-generating sector also has an important role to play: it can accelerate a transition to renewables, replacing coal and peat in particular and redirecting work into new activities centred on renewable energy and, in some cases, deep retrofitting of buildings, starting with those in public ownership.

The wind sector has the potential to generate significant additional employment. Opportunities can equally be found in the 'smart-grid' sector and insulation of existing housing stock, which would reduce fuel poverty and improve the quality of people's lives.

A stronger all-island economy would position Ireland as a key location for investment, trade and labour mobility. Trading on our natural resources and advantages including excellence, safety and 'green' food as well as a strategic investment in renewable energy could make for greater self-sufficiency.

Driving sectoral productivity

An industry commission to kick-start analysis, dialogue and implementation of improvements at sectoral level involving a tripartite arrangement of business, worker representatives and public agencies should be established. Such a process of deliberation could feed into a separate series of negotiations on pay and conditions whether at national or enterprise level. An industry commission approach would undertake an in-depth and up-to-date investigation of the strengths, weaknesses, opportunities and threats in a given sector. It would draw on existing or past analysis as well as relevant expertise especially among employees. To be effective such an analysis would have to involve bottom-up participation by employees and businesses in each sector where knowledge, skills and insights could be pooled and shared without prejudice to commercial confidentiality. A strong emphasis would be placed on domestic enterprises, opportunities for start-ups, obstacles to innovation or growth, opportunities for new markets at home or abroad, levels of skills, links to education and training providers and organisational capacity in the sector.

An exercise like this has multiple benefits: examples of good productivity and innovation performance could be developed and made available across sectors and information shared in a way that opens up commercial opportunities and pathways for new sources of enterprise and employment. A supporting network of advice, finance and intelligence back-up would draw in state agencies such as Enterprise Ireland as well as a state investment bank. Any analysis of sectoral needs and planning should be open to a plurality of ownership forms, including small but potentially vibrant worker-owned cooperatives and new micro-level municipal public enterprises established by local authorities and operated on a commercial and accountable basis with direct employee engagement.

Driving much of the new global economy is the activity of the major technology companies using vast amounts of personal and commercial data (e.g. Apple, Facebook, Microsoft). Cross-country efforts are required to constrain the monopolisation of information and accumulation of associated revenues by a small number of operators. Consideration should be given by national governments and the institutions of the European Union to regulate use of data and enable greater access and transparency in the interests of the common good and not just for monopolistic profits. Where possible, public utilities should be established in which individuals and organisations have the right to share data on a secure basis.

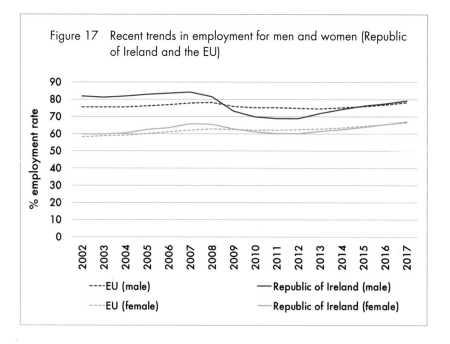

Figure 17 Recent trends in employment for men and women (Republic of Ireland and the EU)

Figure 17 & Figure 18: employment rates are the percentage of a given age-group (20–64 years) in paid employment. Source: Eurostat databank, code [lfsa_ergaed].

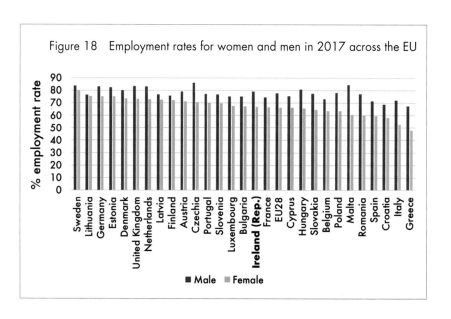

Figure 18 Employment rates for women and men in 2017 across the EU

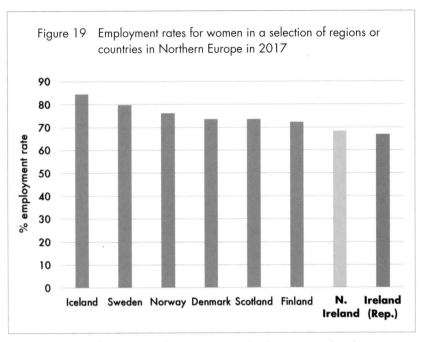

Figure 19   Employment rates for women in a selection of regions or countries in Northern Europe in 2017

Employment rates are the percentage of a given age group (20–64 years) in paid employment. Source: Eurostat databank, code [lfsa_ergaed].

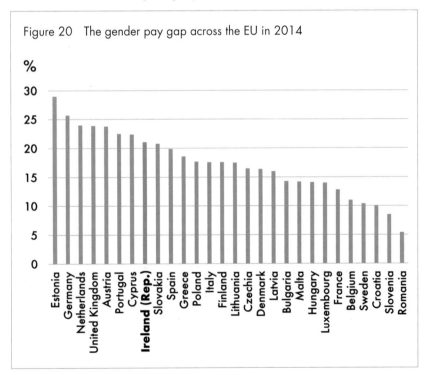

Figure 20   The gender pay gap across the EU in 2014

The gender pay gap is measured by the ratio of the difference between average gross hourly earnings of male and female employees to average gross hourly earnings of male employees. All data refer to the business economy. Source: Eurostat databank, code [earn_gr_gpgr2].

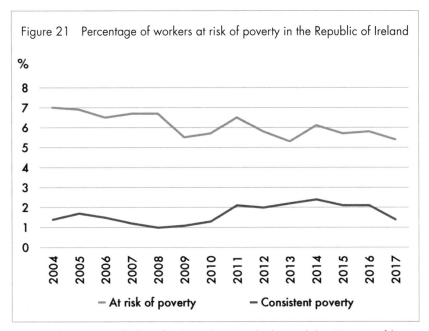

Figure 21 Percentage of workers at risk of poverty in the Republic of Ireland

The at risk of poverty rate is the share of workers with an equivalised income below 60 per cent of the national median income. The consistent poverty rate is the proportion of those both at risk of poverty and who are experiencing enforced deprivation. Source: Central Statistics Office databank, [code SIA14].

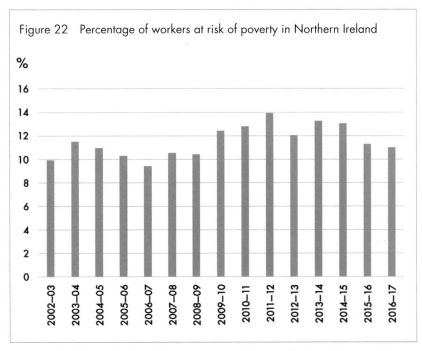

Figure 22 Percentage of workers at risk of poverty in Northern Ireland

Percentage of adults at work in households with an equivalised income of less than 60 per cent of the median income for the UK and after housing costs are taken into account. Source: Family Resources Survey, NISRA and Department for Communities (Northern Ireland).

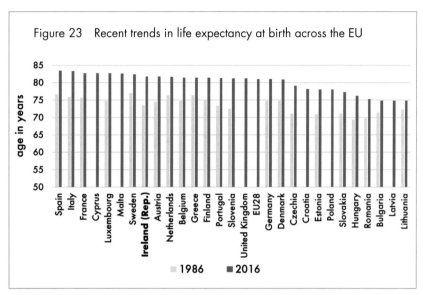

Figure 23 Recent trends in life expectancy at birth across the EU

Germany includes former East Germany in 1986. France data refer to Metropolitan France only in 1986. Data for 1986 are not available for Cyprus, Malta, the UK, Latvia or the EU28. Source: Eurostat databank, code [demo_mlexpec].

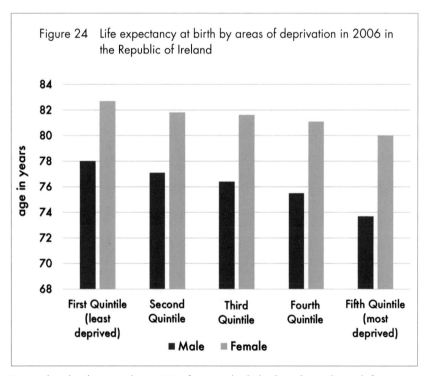

Figure 24 Life expectancy at birth by areas of deprivation in 2006 in the Republic of Ireland

Data are based on the census characteristics of persons who died in the twelve-month period after census night of 23 April 2006. The first quintile is the top 20 per cent of areas *least* deprived and the fifth quintile is the 20 per cent of areas *most* deprived. Source: Central Statistics Office, demographic dataset [PEM01].

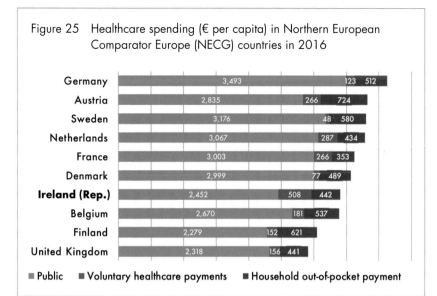

Figure 25   Healthcare spending (€ per capita) in Northern European Comparator Europe (NECG) countries in 2016

Country	Public	Voluntary healthcare payments	Household out-of-pocket payment
Germany	3,493	123	512
Austria	2,835	266	724
Sweden	3,176	48	580
Netherlands	3,067	287	434
France	3,003	266	353
Ireland (Rep.)	2,452	508	442
Belgium	2,670	181	537
Finland	2,279	152	621
United Kingdom	2,318	156	441

■ Public   ■ Voluntary healthcare payments   ■ Household out-of-pocket payment

Healthcare expenditure is measured by the System of Health Accounts. Spending per capita is adjusted for price differences by Eurostat. NECG denotes the Northern European Comparator Group of ten EU member states shown in this figure.

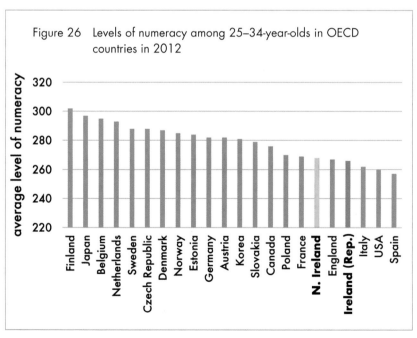

Figure 26   Levels of numeracy among 25–34-year-olds in OECD countries in 2012

Numeracy is measured according to a standard test administered across OECD member countries including some specific regions such as Northern Ireland. Source: Programme for the International Assessment of Adult Competencies (PIAAC) Organisation for Economic Cooperation and Development (http://www.oecd.org/skills/piacc/).

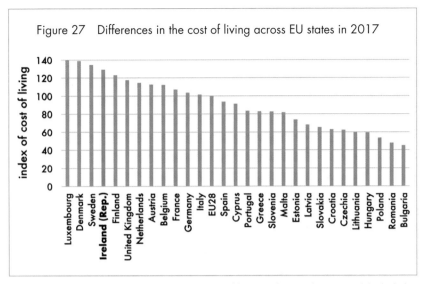

Figure 27   Differences in the cost of living across EU states in 2017

Data are based on actual individual consumption. Cost of living is relative to the EU28 standard which is benchmarked at 100. Source: Eurostat databank [prc_ppp_ind].

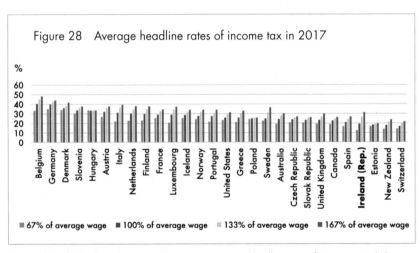

Figure 28   Average headline rates of income tax in 2017

The Republic of Ireland is a low personal income tax country. Headline rates of income tax include social insurance and, in the case of the Republic of Ireland, USC, and apply to single persons only. Rates of tax are as a percentage of wages at four different points in the wage spread from low to average to above average. Countries are ranked according to the average tax rate for average wage taxpayers. Source: OECD online database, *Government at a Glance* [Table 1.5].

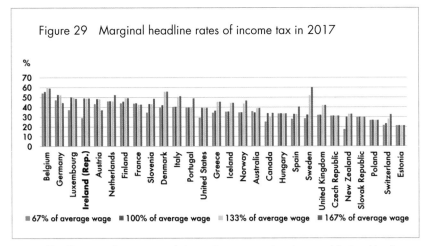

Figure 29   Marginal headline rates of income tax in 2017

Marginal headline rates of income tax include social insurance and, in the case of the Republic of Ireland, USC, and apply to single persons only. Marginal rates of tax are estimated as a percentage of wages at the margin at four different points in the wage spread from low to average to above average. Countries are ranked according to the tax rate for average wage taxpayers. Source: OECD online database, *Government at a Glance* [Table 1.5].

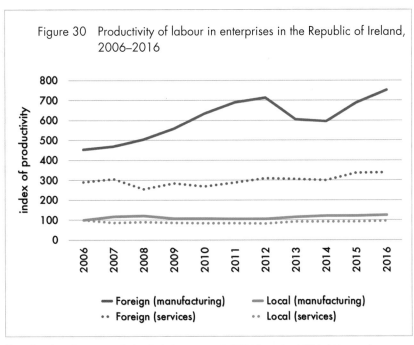

Figure 30   Productivity of labour in enterprises in the Republic of Ireland, 2006–2016

The index of productivity is calculated relative to output in 2006 (based at 100) in Irish-owned enterprises. Source: OECD Economic Survey of Ireland (2018).

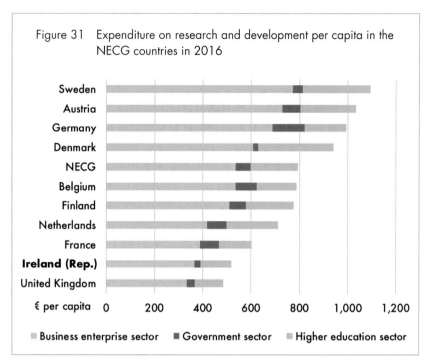

Figure 31   Expenditure on research and development per capita in the NECG countries in 2016

Data are shown as purchasing power standards in constant 2005 prices. Source: Eurostat, intramural R&D expenditure (GERD) by sectors of performance [rd_e_gerdtot].

PART III

WHERE WE GO FROM HERE

9

The Case for Intellectual Promiscuity

Group-think and herding of opinion has been a strong feature of the Irish political economy. If only the prophetic voice of people such as the late UCD economist Professor Patrick Lynch had been heeded in Ireland some of the harm caused in 2008 and later years could have been avoided – or at least ameliorated (Lynch, 1994, p. 168):

> Privatisation is a vogue word today. Too many economists are enthusing about the race towards an unfettered, unrestrained free market economy. This is worship of an unthinking consumerism, animated not by considerations of social responsibility but a desire for the fast buck and let tomorrow look after itself.

The risk of returning to business as usual is as high as ever. Political and business culture has not shifted significantly. Donovan and Murphy (2013, p. 290) have observed that recent developments were 'inevitable by-products of a small country where personal and professional relationships are built up over many years and sharp disagreements may cause friction and upset the smooth functioning of the system'.

The default stance of economics is to assume and never question the existing order of things. Others give the terms of reference:

the economist is a neutral bystander and expert analysts are called on to provide policy options based on the 'evidence' and analysis of the 'facts'. I entirely share the view of Ha-Joon Chang (2014, p. 451):

> Economics is a political argument. It is not – and can never be – a science; there are no objective truths in economics that can be established independently of political, and frequently moral, judgements. Therefore, when faced with an economic argument, you must ask the age-old question '*Cui bono?*' (Who benefits?), first made famous by the Roman statesman and orator Marcus Tullius Cicero.

Economics is often viewed as a positive science that examines choices in a world of constrained resources. One only has so much time or money or capital (including human capital). There are so many choices and needs. The science of economics apparently involves optimising outcomes or well-being by making the most efficient use and allocation of resources. The notion of equity or what we might call social justice is merely given a nod, becoming a footnote in a book or an afterthought at a conference. When pressed on the human reality of market forces, the revered economist declares that it is a distributional or micro matter and one should talk to a micro-economist or specialist in distributional economics and dynamics.

Increasingly, economics has become a term encompassing a vast range of specialisms, each with its own language and preoccupations. What use is economics to public policy and organisational practice? Clearly it must be of some use as governments, banks, trade unions, business organisations, political parties and non-governmental organisations employ economists. Economists frequently occupy a special and privileged role as sages versed in much knowledge and skill in analysing and interpreting the behaviour of individuals, companies and other institutional actors. More than that, economists are not typically shy about offering views and advice on what should be done about many matters ranging from public spending to transport regulation to behavioural incentives in the workplace. The claimed centrality of evidence as a support for public policy marks out economics as a discipline known for its rigour, objectivity and detachment.

Economists are neutral, so it is claimed, especially those working in academia, research foundations or think tanks. This claim is based on the idea that economics is a science involving observation and measurement and, in some cases, experimentation and predictability on the basis of observed and repeated experiments.

Reassessing public policy requires a shift in thinking, discourse and awareness, which itself necessitates thoughtful engagement with those people who wish to join in the conversation. Such a conversation is dependent on a flow of information, research and evidence. This is difficult terrain because too often debate is stultified by a lack of openness to alternative ideas or proposals. We must throw open the windows to allow a cross-pollination of various schools and disciplines. Baert (1998, p. 203) noted the existence of 'a trend among social theorists in the late twentieth century towards avoiding the employment of knowledge from other fields. Instead, quite a number of scholars seem to assume that theoretical progress depends solely on close scrutiny and recycling of preceding social theories.'

Ideas, concepts and practice are frequently at the mercy of various academic or ideological systems. Connecting ideas and concepts advances the work of *synthesis* – not to be confused with *summarising*. Synthesis is about laying different hypotheses and conceptual understandings of the world alongside each other to identify their common pattern and unity alongside their essential difference. There are many ways of telling stories about societies or picturing the complex realities of social relationships. A synthesis helps to connect these different interpretations and thereby inform practice.

It is difficult to start a debate on a vision for the future. Cynicism and inertia are barriers: 'What's the point?', 'What difference does it make?', 'That's been all said and tried before' and

'It's impossible to change people or institutions' are frequent responses to any attempt to start a debate that goes beyond the immediate social and political horizon. Yet there is an urgent need to initiate such a debate and to involve the largest possible audience. Parliament, media and institutions of learning carry out an important role, but additional forums are essential, bringing a wider range of views as well as depth and clarity to these difficult issues. It is difficult to reach the level of depth, listening and engagement required for serious thinking in a parliamentary debate or a television panel discussion. Too often participants in the more traditional forums are eager to prove a point, demolish an opponent or swing public opinion in a particular direction.

Evidence in every form including, but not exclusively, empirical evidence associated with analysis of statistics, is vital to good research. Public policy should be informed by the evidence in relation to how a particular arrangement or policy approach has worked in the past. For this reason, economists employed in the public service, for example, provide an important service to the analysis of data right up to and including the assessment of various policy options. But we do need to guard against two possible fallacies:

- That what is known as the discipline of economics is a full, comprehensive, universal and primary body of knowledge to guide public policy. There are many ways and methods of approaching the complexity of markets and institutions including those offered by such disparate fields as feminist theory, political science, social psychology, neuroscience, ethics, geography, energy studies, planning, philosophy and law.
- That the exercise of economic research can be separated from the specific biases, culture, economic interests and historical context in which it is carried out.

On this latter point we must appreciate that the very research questions we choose to ask, the sources consulted and employed and the audience for which it is written reflects our priorities, our assumptions, our interests, our values and ideological preferences. Honesty must be the hallmark of all research, including in one's ideological or value commitments. Unusual or discomforting facts must be fully acknowledged and pointed out and debated. To declare what we do not know is just as important as to declare or claim what we do, or what we think we do. Economists do not have all the answers and we are not the equivalent of technicians in a laboratory, mixing chemicals or observing the motions of the galaxies. Rather we are creatures of a particular era and fashion of thinking embedded in complex societies and personal histories and hopefully seeking to do an honest job of searching for truth and justice in the world around us. And in that last sentence lies a very explicit value judgement.

Karl Marx, that great political economist, got many things wrong and his followers and disciples got even more things wrong. He famously wrote in his *Theses on Feuerbach*: 'The philosophers have only interpreted the world in various ways; the point, however, is to change it.' Trade unions have the membership and the resources to make a vital difference to adult learning. Trade union education has been an important part of what trade unions have done since the early times. Various initiatives and colleges have been established over the years but these efforts have borne uneven fruit and the recognition and reach of various courses could be better.

Social transformation may occur in a sudden and abrupt way as in various wars, revolutions and rebellions. History has taught us that such disruptions, while bringing temporary improvement and hope, can in many cases lead to new forms of tyranny and disappointing outcomes compared to the initial expectations, hopes and promises.

The most likely and least damaging way of social transformation is through gradual progress, based on as wide a consensus as possible, on the direction of change. This is likely to take two forms or movements, both of which are necessary. One without the other can lead to an ineffective or, worst, still, disastrous result. These are: (i) top down implying the exercise of democratic and accountable political power through the existing or newly emerging structures of government and public institutions; and (ii) bottom up with the emergence of new forms of ownership and participation in countercultural economic and social activity at local and possibly regional level.

Nobody entertaining a vision of social change can be blind to the need for a broad-based political and civil movement to spearhead transformation. In this regard the trade-union movement has a key role to play both in Ireland and internationally. How this movement for change can be brought about so that the positive energies of the largest number of people can be brought together is a major challenge. Existing political movements sympathetic to necessary social change must be on board. We need as broad and inclusive a base as possible, a 'coalition of the willing' extending from trade unions, political parties, faith communities to cultural organisations (see Gold, 2018). Specific alliances with persons or groups who do not share what might be considered a broad progressive agenda are possible and desirable. Even conservatives and neo-liberals can be convinced that effective change to address climate change and provide decent public services is in their interests.

The US activist and academic, George Lakey (2017, p. 252), wrote most usefully in relation to twentieth-century social movements in Sweden and Norway: 'Their creative response had four dimensions: Gaining a rough agreement among the Left on a vision for a new society; using cooperative ownership models to prefigure that vision; practising inclusivity; and, maintaining a commitment to nonviolent struggle.' These insights, surely, have relevance to the current situation in Ireland.

Conor McCabe provides a challenging call in his short pamphlet (McCabe, 2017):

In conclusion, in order to tackle Irish moneyed class interests we need a commonwealth of civil society and trade unions working in tandem with a progressive political sphere. It's about education, campaigns, legislation and resources, all framed by class consciousness – that is, an awareness and understanding of how class works in Ireland, its economic and gendered necessities, and the organisational solidarity needed to tackle it.

McCabe then goes on to say: 'It is entirely achievable.'

10

The Case for Hope

Social change is built on hope. Faced with the biggest ecological crisis threatening the well-being of future generations, we must find ways of engaging the energies, dreams and hopes of a new generation. In his inaugural speech on 26 October 2018, the returning President of Ireland Michael D. Higgins spoke of a new hope for Ireland, for Europe and for the planet 'The people have made a choice as to which version of Irishness they want reflected at home and abroad. It is the making of hope they wish to share rather than the experience of any exploitation of division or fear.'[66]

Part of the challenge facing twenty-first century Ireland is to think in terms of services just as much as cash income; in terms of development as much as in growth in GDP; and in terms of all types of work and not just paid work.

Not helpless

Change is possible and desirable. Too often public debate about choices in public policy is framed around a narrow range of assumptions, givens and permissible questions. A particular set of social arrangements and policy ideas is assumed, implying that following these is fixed and beyond changing: the social welfare system as it evolved in the post-war settlement, the education system as it was conceived in the wake of the industrial revolution, the health system as comprising a large private insurance element in the Republic of Ireland, the labour market as a hierarchy of skilled groups and the political system as we know it.

We need to challenge the idea that existing arrangements are inevitable or beyond public discussion. Huge transformations took place in earlier decades, including the opening up of the economy of the Republic of Ireland in the 1960s against a background of outright opposition in some cases and apathy and disengagement in others. Change does not happen by accident. Leadership, opportunity, ideas, example from abroad, example from within and force of events and the tide of global swings can have a profound influence on public policy and social outcomes.

In a recent essay Dr Fergus O'Ferrall (O'Hanlon, 2017, p. 54) draws on the political philosophy of civic republicanism: 'We should not be afraid to reimagine together the whole Irish democratic republican project. Achieving a truly Irish civic republic shaped by solidarity, community active citizenship will demand no less.'

O'Ferrall raises the idea of not only a national civic forum (such as, for example, the Citizen's Assembly) but the suggestion of locally-based civic forums in each county and city in Ireland. This should, in my view, extend to Northern Ireland, where such forums could complement the political process and give voice to communities that are marginalised as well as those distanced from each other.

What does the future hold for capitalism as we know it? Many varieties of capitalism discussed so far have evolved over time. I have frequently referenced the Nordic Model as a form of political economy adapted to the global and internal market economy but compatible with a strong social safety network as well as proactive public policies that ensure a more equal distribution of income as well as a provision of particular public goods, 'free' or heavily subsidised at the point of use.

Imagining a future Europe and Ireland's place within it demands something more than a rehash of yesterday's ideas and plans. For a vision to make sense and to attract popular support it must meet the following criteria:

- something like it has been successfully tried before;
- something like it exists now and seems to be working;
- a critical mass of people believe that moving on from where we are to something better is not only possible but desirable.

The above may seem trite and banal yet the difficulty confronting many on the left is that it appears that a majority of people living in Ireland do not trust those who might advocate a radical departure from capitalism 'as we know it'. A supposed halfway house of the Nordic Model or social democracy is attractive to some but poorly understood by most people. In any case there is no one Nordic Model and Scandinavian countries have been under severe strain despite their various models since the 1980s, if not earlier. Still, the experience of those countries in the latter half of the twentieth century is valuable and instructive. One is pushed to cite a better model and experience in the last 100 years, combining as it does relatively low levels of social inequality, high levels of productivity and living standards together with high levels of education, health and well-being. It is still capitalism – albeit with a more human face – and a good compromise that kept most Scandinavians on side.

But would such a model work on the island of Ireland? There is no reason it should not. Frequent objections or doubts are raised on the grounds of national political culture: antipathy to paying more tax; and the dictates of EU or global market constraints.

The first objection is not convincing. All the Scandinavian countries underwent enormous changes following the bleak and highly conflictual 1930s. The Nordic Model was not an accident: it was the product of specific factors and external influences and threats, not least from the East. There is no reason why the impossible and the unthinkable could not happen here in Ireland but it may take a generation or more to build the momentum with a strong and courageous leadership. This is where the trade union movement, in particular, has a role to play.

The second objection concerning global pressure is a more serious challenge. It might have been possible to build socialism behind tariff walls and other controls in the past. Economies are too global, capital too free and information too borderless for the likelihood of any project to establish a completely different social arrangement within a sovereign national unit. This partly explains the enthusiasm of some labour movement activists to achieve 'more Europe', by which they mean closer monetary, fiscal and policy integration across the European Union *but* (crucially) a strong added 'social' element in the form of progressive laws and practices to develop public services, protect labour rights and sustain the environment. That is an important *but*.

We have a choice. The risks associated with a global fall in the share of total national income going to labour as well as rising inequality in wages and other incomes is that the rich will continue to get richer, the poor will continue to be poor, communities will remain cut off and impoverished and political power will drift to the global centres of finance capital and unaccountable supra-national intergovernmentalism. Meanwhile individuals and families continue to pay a high price for the follies of unbridled capitalism, which placed profit before people, rights of capital before rights of labour, property before homes and the fiscal rules of austerity before human rights.

The Republic of Ireland faces a challenge in navigating the troubled waters of a changing and fragile political economy in Europe and the UK. In the case of the Republic of Ireland, further political, banking and fiscal integration into the European Union would severely constrain its policy discretion while in Northern Ireland there is very limited scope to raise taxes or undertake large-scale public investment and enterprise development given the current political impasse and disruption likely to result from

Brexit. The situation facing both jurisdictions should not distract from the potential to effect significant social and economic progress over coming decades especially if global circumstances prove to be positive and political and social movements in Ireland work effectively with others in Europe.

In many ways the unfinished business of the democratic revolution proclaimed a century ago is the goal of social equality and true emancipation. Today we see a rise in homelessness, precarious and low-paid work, the scandal of zero-hour or if-and-when contracts and the corrosive effect and wastage of skills and capabilities of long-term youth unemployment and underemployment in much of Europe.

Attainment of full employment and a living income for all will require fundamental change in society. It will not be possible to reach a position of sustainable growth in well-being without a democratic transformation of economic and political institutions. This must encompass a shift in relationships of ownership, control and civic engagement. A paper produced by the Northern Ireland Public Service Alliance (2013, p. 17) makes the case for a radical alternative:

> This means that, in dealing with these issues, the argument we make for democratic control in our anti-privatisation fight, for example, will have another consequence. It is to initiate a wider debate on the sort of society in which we want to live. This will mean the trade union movement advancing an alternative economic and political strategy, to the neoliberalism being foisted upon us. We know it cannot be about a more benign form of capitalism as it is clear that such an idea is an illusion. Therefore, it will have to be about us arguing for an economy that we own, a socialist economy that is fully democratic, that plans in order to meet the needs of our people, and that operates in solidarity with our local, national and international allies.

The Constitution of the Irish Congress of Trade Unions reminds us of the following:

> To seek the full utilisation of the resources of Ireland for the benefit of the people of Ireland and to work for such fundamental changes in the social and economic system as will secure for the workers of Ireland adequate and effective participation in the control of the industries and services in which they are employed.[67]

Civil society organisations, including trade unions, have a vital role not only in defending workers' rights and conditions but in advancing a social programme to change Ireland into a more economically dynamic, socially equal and politically accountable place: the best small egalitarian country in the world, in which every child is cherished and can flourish. The better is yet to come, but it must be worked for.

The role of ecological, feminist and other movements is also important. These speak to important and vital areas of human emancipation and should not be reduced to wheels in some other chariot.

Being ready for the 'national question'

'The EU needs to prepare for a united Ireland,' said former Taoiseach Enda Kenny in July 2016, some weeks following the UK referendum on Brexit. Clearly, the mood in the Republic of Ireland and Northern Ireland has changed if only because particular questions are being asked in places and among people where formerly such questions were seen as taboo or irrelevant. The process of British disengagement from the EU combined with the Belfast Agreement has changed the game. Four into three does not go. We cannot have frictionless trade on an east-west or north-south basis alongside UK departure from the European Union customs union and single market. Compromises, delays and temporary arrangements including special arrangements for Northern Ireland may be possible but the day of reckoning cannot be postponed indefinitely. The current dispensation is simply not sustainable in the long run.

The question of Irish unity has raised its head even among sections of the population that might never have considered it a possibility in their lifetime. Three possible responses come to mind:

- Everything should be done to keep Northern Ireland fully in the UK even at the cost of some considerable disruption regarding the 'four freedoms' (applicable to goods, services, people and capital) on the North-South interface between the UK and the EU. That interface stretches 499 kilometres from Carlingford Lough to Lough Foyle. The point is that no territory can be in two different customs unions or associated regulatory markets. This is the view of many in the unionist community in Northern Ireland including some who voted to remain in the EU.
- Irish reunification is the only feasible response to the chaos and division likely to flow from Brexit. This in combination with demographic change makes unity not only likely but highly desirable and necessary. This is the view of many Irish nationalists, including members of the Irish parliament who contributed to the 2017 report on unity (Houses of the Oireachtas, 2017b).
- Irish reunification seems unavoidable in the long run because of demographic change coupled with the very likely disruptive and economically negative impacts of Brexit. But it will take a long time to put in place and requires enthusiastic support and cooperation from a large majority on both sides of the border. This seems to correspond to the views of many who do not readily sign up to one of the first two positions.

Of the three responses, the first two involves protagonists making the case for change of one sort or another. If the argument is made for retaining full incorporation into the UK then the Belfast Agreement is not the same as it was understood to be in 1998. The main difference is that the existence of a common market and set of market rules were simply assumed when that agreement was reached but will no longer operate in the future if Brexit is fully applied. Protagonists for a united Ireland have widespread support in both parts of Ireland and their case is likely to be strengthened if economic events turn even more sour in Northern Ireland as may very well be the case.[68] However, the extent of opposition to Irish unity should not be underestimated if anything is known about the legacy of the Troubles that traumatised Northern Ireland for over three decades. Moreover, the contested area of the potential fiscal cost of a united Ireland facing taxpayers in the Republic of Ireland cannot be dismissed on the grounds that reunification will transform both economies so rapidly as to cancel out any adverse costs associated with integration of Northern Ireland into a united Ireland.

In 2017 the Joint Committee of the Oireachtas published a comprehensive report on the Implementation of the Good Friday Agreement, recommending a pathway towards Irish unity. The report also cites research evidence prepared in advance of the report by a number of academics (Houses of the Oireachtas, 2017b).

One thing is sure: the debate will not go away. While much of it will be conducted on the basis of interpretation of the economic facts together with hypothetical scenarios, more of it will be about identity, memory, fears and hopes. I believe that a much healing of hearts and minds is necessary before political reconciliation is possible but will take a very long time. However, I may be proven wrong. Who, in 1912, who would have imagined Ireland in 1922?

The national question concerns not only the relationship between the islands of Great Britain and Ireland but also the relationships among people resident and rooted on the island of Ireland. Historical legacy, divergent identities and communal belonging as well as divergent political and economic pathways have brought about a partition of mentalities on the island of which institutional borders are more a symptom than a cause.

Important historical reasons for the attachment to the union with Great Britain for the majority of people living in Northern Ireland (many of whom are members of trade unions, which for historical reasons are part of an all-Ireland congress) include cultural identity and attachment (based on language, religion, ethnicity, etc.), denominational affiliation (as a key dividing fact from the Reformation/Counter-Reformation onwards), European politics (with all of its rivalries and intrigue) and economic considerations (the perceived benefits of being part of a union of Ireland and Great Britain).

All these factors were highly relevant during the decade leading up to 1922. Partition seemed inevitable once Home Rule became a serious proposal from 1912 onwards. With the passage of time and dramatic changes in the global and UK economies as well as in cultural and religious changes (especially in the Republic of Ireland) it is less evident that these factors are as relevant today, if at all. However, the depth of attachment to the union and the extent of opposition to any change in this arrangement should not be underestimated by Irish nationalists. Moreover, any prospects of reunification later in this century will not be in any way assisted by the use of physical force or similar threats.

Aside from the above, some events may potentially completely change the context: take Scottish independence, or another disruptive or completely unforeseen development.

Beware of black swans

Nobody can predict our future beyond pointing to the inexorable evidence of climate change and ageing societies and the disruptive impact of new technologies. Thus, we find ourselves living with many black swans, from the rise of various populisms to the inherent instability of the global financial system; events that come as surprises, have major effects and are often rationalised after the fact with the benefit of hindsight.

However, catastrophism has been proven generally wrong – at least so far. Capitalism survived and flourished and large sections of the working classes, however defined, bought into the prevailing order by virtue of economic status or share in capitalism. However, if the catastrophists and prophets of the imminent collapse of capitalism have been proven wrong, then so have the cheerleaders and apologists for the existing order. The systematic, large-scale and dramatic collapse in banking, investment, trade and output of 2008–10 was not meant to happen. Such sharp swings in the global economy had been abolished according to the proponents of the great moderation. The internal contradictions and inherent instability of capitalism – especially in its new incarnation as a highly financialised, global and information driven system – were laid bare. And it was not a pretty sight.

The Greek crisis of 2012–15 showed that the new euro currency membership zone is not irreversible. The rise of aggressive and beggar-thy-neighbour nationalism demonstrates that free trade, peace, parliamentary democracy and free speech cannot be taken for granted. The triumph of intergovernmentalism and the copper-fastening of the fiscal rules make it clear that 'social Europe' is not inevitable. The volatility in political sentiment in almost every advanced economy and Western society shows that nothing can be assumed. The speed at which the great moderation of consistent growth, low interest rates and full employment came crashing down in 2008 in a matter of weeks proves that extreme events in the business cycle are not outside of history and there is no law that they can only happen once every few decades. For example, extreme seasonal and climatic conditions are consistent with the undeniable scientific evidence that the planet is changing due to human behaviour in ways that may be just as threatening as nuclear annihilation.

One of the most important lessons from recent Irish history is that the unthinkable becomes thinkable and the unexpected will happen while the expected very often does not. Why should the future be any different in this regard to the past? The last thirty years have seen the fall of the Berlin Wall, the collapse of the Soviet Union, the transformation of China, the end of apartheid in South Africa and the resolution (for now) of the Troubles in Northern Ireland. Anybody who predicted any or all of these developments as recently as the late 1980s would have been dismissed as delusional. Similarly, an expectation or projection that population would increase to over 6.8 million on the island of Ireland in 2016, that GDP per capita would be among the highest in the European Union, that a sustained period of growth, prosperity, and movement towards 'full employment' and peace in Northern Ireland was about to arrive from the mid-1990s onwards might have been consigned to the category of summer school madness.

The period 2008–10 provides a very graphic example of a black swan event in Irish banking. The worst-case scenario cited by the UCD economist, Morgan Kelly, involved €25 billion in impaired banking assets, an estimate that was derided as late as September 2008.

Black swans may appear as benign, such as the historically unprecedented increase in GDP in 2015 reported by the CSO in July 2016 on foot of revisions to previous estimates. In the latter case, the black swan was accounted for by publicly anonymous corporations re-classifying the legal ownership status of their global operations for strategic reasons of avoiding or minimising tax. Whether this benign occurrence by way of a one-off increase in the level of GDP is sustained for the coming decade is not known. This particular swan could become nasty if the same corporations switched legal classifications of their global operations away from Ireland leaving the Republic of Ireland, in possibly the largest statistical recession in GDP in its history.

The best we can do is to work for the best, be prepared for the worst and always expect the unexpected. Specifically, every policy initiative needs to be vetted against an expected drop in revenue or economic activity. Worst-case scenarios should be part of regular budgetary planning. Greater honesty and openness in relation to future economic developments should characterise public debate and policy deliberation.

Socialism in our time?

The US presidential elections in 2016 proved that the word socialism is now an acceptable term to use even if people hasten to add adjectives such as 'democratic' or 'ecological' to curtail any misunderstanding. McDonnell (2018, p. xvii) writes, 'We are seeking nothing less than to build a society that is radically fairer, more democratic and more sustainable, in which the wealth of society is shared by all. The historic name for that society is socialism.'

At its simplest, socialism is a set of ideas and principles that much of economic activity should be conducted by organisations that are publicly or community owned and directed. In other words, the ownership and control of production, distribution and exchange is socialised. In practice, elements of private-for-profit, private-not-for-profit, state-for-profit and state-not-for-profit organisations exist in a mixed economy of ownership types. Elements of socialisation may be introduced into mainly private or capitalistically run enterprises (such as, for example, worker-directors in state-owned enterprises in the Republic of Ireland in the 1970s). There are many combinations and shades of practice in between capitalism and socialism, depending on local culture and inherited institutions and structures of economic activity.

Understood in this way, socialism does not necessarily imply state ownership of the 'commanding heights' of the economy. But it does assert the primacy of public goods and interests over those of private interests or profit-seeking corporations as was envisaged in the Democratic Programme a century ago. Such an assertion of public interest must be subject to democratic norms and rules and not concentrated in the hands of a small elite unaccountable or unelected or both. If the latter were the case then socialism would represent a replacement of one form of rule by the elite with another form.

The test of socialism (or any other 'ism') is in its capacity to deliver the three Ps:

- peace as in the absence of war and its causes as well as all forms of violence and institutional abuse;
- prosperity as in having the freedom to use resources and enjoy life in conformity with one's values as a member of a community;
- protection of fundamental human rights, including emancipation by reason of sex, race and religion.

The failure of socialism in countries such as the USSR, China and other central and Eastern European countries has had a profound impact on thinking and public discourse. Ireland is no exception. The fact that millions died as a result of authoritarian dictatorships in the former communist states and that living standards and human freedoms were severely curtailed cannot be denied (the superb German TV series *Deutschland 83* and *86* is a timely reminder for a generation that never knew the Cold War and what life was like on both side of the divide in Europe). But it cannot be denied that some positive lessons were learned in former communist states and the very existence of such states and associated ideology had a profoundly positive (as well as negative) effect on the evolution of social policy in Western Europe and beyond. In simple terms, the ruling classes of the West were so scared of communist contagion in Western Europe that various adaptations of capitalism and application of Keynesian economic approaches were *de rigueur* for about thirty years after the catastrophe of World War II.

The period 1945–73 along with the heyday of European social democracy, especially in Scandinavia, was a carefully and pragmatically constructed class compromise involving a measure of redistribution, social control and public services required to ensure cohesion in the face of the very real threat from the East. The establishment of the ECSC, which later became the European Union, was in part a response to an attempt to build a capitalist trade block informed by liberal, social and Christian democratic values. It was the answer of the West to COMECON,[69] led by the USSR prior to its collapse in 1991. However, the roots of closer European cooperation and even federalism predate the end of World War II, as drawn up in the Ventotene Manifesto by Altiero Spinelli and Ernesto Rossi while they were prisoners on the Italian island of Ventotene in 1941.

The exercise of power is different in any given social arrangement. A statist model founded on ownership and control of means of production by a state in turn controlled by a political elite provides a concrete social model which, at its height in the 1980s, encompassed a third of humanity. Communism continues in only a handful of states these days and is unlikely to re-emerge any time in the near future. There is hardly any support for the application of such a model in Ireland.

A variation on the statist model is the application of democratic principles to the exercise of political power in a predominantly state-owned economy. This was, to some degree, true of the attempted – and unsuccessful – Hungarian and Czech reforms in 1956 and 1968, respectively. Partly as a consequence of this the level of popular support for such a radical model is limited not only in Ireland but in other countries as well. The maxim of 'be careful what you wish for' is applicable here.

The development of various forms of compromise built on the foundation of a market economy but incorporating many key social interventions found under socialism is the end result of various social experiments during the twentieth century. Social democracy is characterised by a strong role for the state and, in some cases, voluntary associations (for example trade unions in Denmark) in regulating the economic activities of companies and other organisations for the common good. But the essential make up of existing social democracy is a variant of capitalism with a strong concentration of economic power in the hands of private corporations as well as an element of compromise in the role of workers and other actors in exercising social control over economic life. The social democratic experiment has undergone very significant change and retrenchment in the face of global pressures.

Are there yet other forms of ownership, control and polity that stand outside or within the known models of capitalism or socialism? Wright (2013) discusses, in an abstract way, a number of other 'isms' and models that combine strong elements of bottom-up social power and influence, especially with reference to worker- or community-owned cooperatives as well as forms of democratic deliberation and street assemblies that have proven successful in some places. However, the dearth of concrete examples that have (i) demonstrably worked, (ii) are extensive and large-scale in application and not just limited to micro-level examples, and (iii) could be applied on a wide scale in both parts of the island of Ireland seem wanting. This is as much the case now as it was in 1864 or, in 1919, when the Democratic Programme was released.

Yet capitalism has changed dramatically over the last 200 years and various permutations, adaptations and transformations have been useful and valid. The use of Keynesian macroeconomic management proved decisive in economic recovery and business cycle regulation during the thirty years following World War II, for example. The role of a strong and innovative partnership role for the state and civil society in the Nordic countries holds lessons for everyone, even today. The rise of the info-economy and the transformation in knowledge production and dissemination has had a dramatic and generally positive impact on lives since the 1990s.

The world has become a lot more messy than it was under a binary world of capitalism and socialism.[70] Everyone is for democracy and democratic values until these values get in the way of a particular interest or agenda. For all its imperfections universal suffrage, parliamentary elections and the right to periodic recall at least once every five years are important and hard-won gains for citizens. Together with a free and genuinely open media, neither controlled by the state or monopolised by one or two private corporations, democracy in the legal and political sphere is an important but not sufficient condition for the achievement of equality of treatment for citizens. Participation in economic and social affairs including those of commercial enterprises is a central contributing factor to equality. In an increasingly globalised economy decisions made by boards or intergovernmental institutions in faraway places determine the outcomes for workers and communities in a way that is sometimes brutal and unjust.

What we need is plurality of strategies to replace the dominance of capitalist power relations with various experiments and initiatives from worker cooperatives to mutual credit unions and social economy projects in which principles of democracy, equality and sustainability replace or supplement the driving principle of profit. There is a role for state power – democratised and subjected to social power, which can play an important role in supporting various forms of what may be termed anti-capitalist initiative. However, the idea of a revolutionary rupture accompanied by a state takeover to nationalise the 'commanding heights of the economy' is not on the agenda today and is hardly likely to be in this century given the experience of the last one. We might conceive counter-capitalist bounded projects such as in social economy, worker cooperatives and various 'commons' projects from time-sharing to information-sharing or demarcation of urban gardens.

McCabe (2013) points out that, while welcome, these examples do not in themselves constitute a strategy to transform society from capitalism into something else. Rather, these examples need to form part of a more explicitly political strategy to wrestle with state power and class relations. We live in a global finance system where global financial interests exercise enormous power over social and economic conditions throughout the world. Only a collective mobilisation of labour can contest this power in the battleground of ideas, political power and workplaces. In this regard McCabe underlines the potential role of trade unions as organisations that can mobilise large numbers of workers and set a political direction for change – in association with other progressive civil society organisations.

An important distinction must be drawn between social democracy and democratic socialism although these terms may seem interchangeable. Moreover, the very meaning of these terms has undergone change to such an extent that an early twentieth-century socialist such as Jim Larkin or James Connolly could not have imagined the rise and fall of communism in what was, in their time, a very backward part of Europe. Neither could they have imagined the transformation of capitalism, the rise of a new concept and practice of social democracy as a historical compromise and amelioration of the worst effects of capitalism. The metamorphism in European social democracy, understood as a broad left-of-centre political movement, into political expressions more akin to social and liberal movements against which classical twentieth-century social democracy were pitted has changed the political landscape. Terms such as 'left' and 'right', 'liberal' and 'neo-liberal', 'socialist' and 'social democratic' do not mean the same things at different points in modern history or even in different places across the world.

The renewed rise of 'socialism' as a term and its adoption by leaders such as Jeremy Corbyn and Bernie Sanders has made it somewhat more respectable, at least in the UK and the US. The threats of red scaremongering has less appeal than it might have in the past for a number of reasons, not least because the 'spectre of communism' no longer haunts Europe, to borrow a phrase from Karl Marx.

New social democracy as it refers to large-scale political movements and parties in Europe defines a movement to change and reform capitalism by emphasising equality, public services, workers' rights and the principles of political democracy and participation. New social democracy differs from liberal or other forms of democratic politics by virtue of its emphasis and priorities. In practice, new social democratic politics has increasingly moved into a defensive position of seeking to protect particular gains or institutions from the never-ending encroachment of the market and fiscal conservatism. In some cases, (e.g. under the New Labour period in the United Kingdom) 'social democracy' consciously discarded any notion of a radical change in society and in the ownership of the means of production. It effectively carried forward or maintained the reforms brought in by conservative governments in relation to the labour market, ownership of utilities and the introduction of market principles into areas such as education and health. In this regard the UK expression of social democracy was not significantly different from those in other key European societies such as Germany or Italy. As for Eastern and much of Central Europe, new social democracy has been so weakened as to be relegated to a role of political irrelevance, at least for now.

If the essence of social democracy is reform of capitalism and protection of past gains, the essence of democratic socialism is very different. Democratic socialism (a term extensively used in social democratic movements and by politicians such as Corbyn and Sanders) implies a more radical and fundamental change in the economic and social order but one also in which the democracy is fully preserved and even deepened by widening access to ownership and control of key economic decisions. The traditional fault line between left and right centred on the issue of ownership – whether or not the state or public and community organisations should own, direct and control key economic resources or whether private enterprise should do this – is likely to shift again. This time, it may shift to a fault line between social democracy and democratic socialism on the key issue of ownership. Democratic socialism aims at a central and lead role for the state and for community and cooperative ventures to dominate in the production of goods and services. This does not preclude a strong role for private enterprises in directing economic activity, but the balance shifts from private corporate actors to public and community ones.

Does democratic socialism exist anywhere? I believe that it is unlikely that democratic socialism ever existed anywhere in a real, meaningful and sustained way. It certainly did not exist at any stage of the history of the USSR from 1917 to 1990. This is also the case in countries that applied the doctrines and practices of the USSR. The key missing ingredient was democracy – whatever about the extent to which socialism was ever really undertaken in communist regimes. Neither can it be claimed that the generally successful social democratic countries in Scandinavia are socialist. They are democracies in the sense that the term is used even in the limited sense of representative or parliamentary democracy, but they were and remain mainly market economies, led in the main by private companies but with significant elements of state influence and engagement (although less so now than in the past).

So, if democratic socialism has never existed anywhere long enough to be assessed, how can anyone know that it would represent an improvement on the existing social and economic order? Moreover, why would the general public and broad trade union membership trust a democratic socialist policy or movement if one were created in Ireland as well as elsewhere? The best answer is that we do not know for sure. What we do know is that capitalism has failed to curb the trashing of the earth and with it the risks to survival of our species. It has also failed to prevent widespread poverty and inequality across the globe. We can do better than this.

It is difficult to say what prospects a democratic socialist transformation would have in Ireland, Europe and the world, but attempts at reforming capitalism have not worked and are unlikely to do so, given the scale of the environmental, technological and demographic challenges. Judging by historical experience, any attempt to bring about positive and lasting social transformation will fail if (i) it is imposed from above, as happened in the USSR, China and other places and (ii) it is attempted in one country or region only. Economies are too global and interconnected to allow for self-contained social experiments. Moreover, without lasting and popular support and direction, from-the-top social-ism is doomed to failure as the lessons of the USSR and associated regimes demonstrated.

Rapid changes in patterns of ownership characterise recent decades on the island of Ireland, as part of a global trend away from state ownership towards private or mixed public-private ownership. At the same time, production and ownership of the means of production has become more concentrated. Decisions regarding investment, production or location of economic activity are at a remove from the workplace and national and public domains.

A shared set of human values should be at the heart of Ireland's economy and society. These values might stem from dif-ferent sources and philosophies but all unite on the fundamental principles, which include the right to life and personal safety, accommodation, gainful and decent employment, education and health, participation in the democratic process and the right to belong to a trade union and to engage in collective bargaining.

There is an urgent need for coordination by all concerned to meet the three main demographic, technological and envi-ronmental challenges and to enhance the well-being of society. Employment is essential in providing the means to enable people to realise well-being but the organisation of work in enterprises needs to drive an increase in productivity that is smart and ecologically sound. This is the future of work and the future of enterprises if Ireland is to gain a stronger foothold in global production chains. Key to a high-productivity and ecologically balanced pattern of life is the role of public goods and services, especially in the vital areas of health, education and transport. Future prosperity and distribution of life chances for the next generation depends crucially on three big goals: the realisation of quality employment based on 'work that pays'; access to public services including housing, education and health; and development of enterprises that can provide the employment, income and revenue streams to invest in these public goods.

Incredible patience

This book makes the case for a vision of a vibrant, inclusive and outward-looking participatory economy with a strong component of state-led innovation and universal public services, free at the point of use. In summary, making this vision a reality requires:

- a strong leading role for the state in driving innovation, finance and enterprise;
- development of a state banking system alongside an expanded countrywide people's bank for small to medium-sized savers/ borrowers and businesses;
- significantly higher levels of taxes on incomes and consumption, especially on those most able to afford such taxes to pay for universal public services for a growing and diverse population;
- a fundamental and irreversible shift in patterns of production and consumption to render Ireland carbon-free by 2050;
- a root-and-branch reform of public and private sectors to make all medium and large enterprises more accountable to society, workers and communities.

Such ideas and policies – although not socialism as we know it – could point us in a new direction that transcends the polarities and dualism of the past. Concluding thoughts (author's italics) are left to Irish political economist and historian Dr Conor McCabe (2013, p. 51): 'The process of building a new society is a dull revolution, incremental in nature, requiring *incredible patience*. It also requires a *plan*.'

Towards a New Democratic Programme

Reinventing and saving the European Union

- Establish a European Insurance Social Fund based on a 1 per cent levy on all member states. This fund would pay for training and income of EU workers made redundant over a fixed period of time.
- Establish a European Climate Fund based on a community carbon tax applied across all member states at a rate of 1 per cent of GDP. This fund would be used to invest in renewable energy and interconnectors to peripheral states as well as public transport.
- The EU should take up a 'Marshall Plan for Europe' as advocated by the German trade unions. This could be funded by a European-wide financial transactions tax and would target green public transport across the union.

Taking work seriously

- Impose a cap of €0.5 million euro on top salaries in the private sector. This could be part of a new social contract: the ratio of top pay to the minimum and the median should not exceed an agreed European-wide norm. A high pay commission should monitor and advise on norms for high pay in particular sectors, including banking.
- Roll out a guaranteed work or training programme at EU level beginning with a programme applied to persons under 30 years of age.
- A target rate of employment (20–64-year-olds) of 80 per cent by 2025 on the island of Ireland.
- Extend paid parental leave up to six months to be set at 80 per cent of sick pay levels. This could be paid, in part, from a European social insurance fund.
- Outlaw zero-hour contracts across the island of Ireland and ensure a right to a stable level of working hours supplemented, if necessary by paid training leave.

- Action to better monitor and understand the gender pay gap and identify sectoral and enterprise specific areas where follow-up is required.
- Provide stronger legal and constitutional rights for collective bargaining and trade union membership.
- Raise the minimum wage to 60 per cent of median earnings by 2025 across the island of Ireland.
- Put in place a more effective labour market monitoring system to root out bad employment practice and failure to comply with legal standards.
- Aim for 95 per cent rates of educational attainment equivalent to upper secondary or higher among the adult population by 2030 across the island of Ireland.

Taking the social wage seriously

- Introduce a European Cost Rental Model for the Republic of Ireland. This would offer the option of secure, affordable and quality rental accommodation to a mix of households. A public commercial company – to be called The Housing Company of Ireland – could work alongside the Northern Ireland Housing Executive.
- In line with the *Sláintecare Report*, a universal healthcare system modelled along European lines to provide a top-class cradle-to-grave healthcare service on the basis of need and not ability to pay.
- Invest in a public transport system fit for a population of ten million on the island and operating on a zero-carbon basis.
- Provide a lifelong learning plan to work with the grain of the brain by providing a greater mix of theoretical, applied and workplace-based learning. This plan should ensure that everyone is equipped to keep on learning no matter what age they are.
- Create a People's Fund to subsume the existing 'rainy day fund' and the social insurance fund. This would be an active and dynamic fund driving innovation and meeting long-term social needs.
- Raise and hold public spending at 45 per cent of modified national income by 2025.

- Begin a stepwise increase in social insurance in the Republic of Ireland over a 10-year period to reach EU norms to pay for pensions and income during periods of reduced participation in the labour market. The first step should include a targeted increase in employer social insurance contribution in respect of earnings by the top 10 per cent of wage earners.
- In Northern Ireland use whatever limited revenue-raising discretion exists to reform local property taxes to pay for local infrastructural projects, including investment in alternative energy sources.

Taking tax reform seriously

- We need a root-and-branch reform of taxation.
- Prioritise an accelerated plan to increase community carbon taxes up to 2025.
- Simplify the income tax code by removing unnecessary tax reliefs and introducing a range of tax rates with a more gradual increase in personal tax (rather than the cliff-edge effect on the threshold between the lower and higher rates).
- Apply a minimum effective rate of 5 per cent to corporate income.
- Review local property and other capital taxes with the aim of increasing tax yield.

Taking enterprise seriously

- Protect the single electricity market and associated regulatory framework on the island.
- Open up a greater diversity of enterprise ownership models and remove some of the legal obstacles.
- Set up and recognise Companies of Excellence based on criteria of employee participation, compliance with sustainable goals and limitation on pay differentials within enterprises.
- Keep public investment pegged at 5 per cent of national income. Raise total R&D spend to 5 per cent of national income. Aim for a 3 per cent retraining budget at enterprise level. Establish an all-island development bank to support SMEs in transition to new markets.

- Establish a community-owned third force bank giving greater choice and competition to the big players in banking.
- A just transition will require new and alternative sources of energy to replace existing coal and peat-burning stations.
- Consider an industry commission with sectoral branches to kick-start analysis, dialogue and implementation of improvements at sectoral level.

Diversity of ideas, hope and action

Economics need to give way to political economy. Anything less will fail to address the scale of the environmental challenge before us. Many roads are possible. We need to learn from the past and not be held prisoner to it. We might yet be prisoners of hope.

List of Figures

Sources

Atkinson, Anthony (2015) *Inequality – What Can Be Done?* Cambridge, Massachusetts: Harvard University Press.

Baert, Patrick (1998) *Social Theory in the Twentieth Century*. Cambridge, UK: Polity Press.

Baker, John, Kathleen Lynch, Sara Cantillon and Judy Walsh (2009) *Equality: From Theory to Action*. London: Palgrave Macmillan.

Barry, John (2018) 'Towards a Sustainable Economy: Ideas, Ideology, Institutions and "Letting Go to Move on"'. Online paper, https://www.academia.edu/36837154/Towards_a_Sustainable_Economy_-_Ideas_Ideology_Institutions_and_letting_go_to_move_on_, accessed 11 March 2019. Belfast: Queen's University Belfast.

Begg, David (2016) *Ireland, Small Open Economies and European Integration: Lost in Transition*. London: Palgrave Macmillan.

Bradley, John and Michael Best (2012) *Cross-Border Economic Renewal: Rethinking Regional Policy in Ireland*. Armagh: Centre for Cross-Border Studies.

Central Bank of Ireland (2015) *Credit Money and Banking Statistics – Business Credits and Deposits*. Dublin: Central Bank of Ireland.

Central Statistics Office (2015a) *European Household Finance and Consumption Survey 2013*. Dublin: Central Statistics Office.

Central Statistics Office (2017) *Sustainable Development Indicators Ireland 2017*. Dublin: Central Statistics Office.

Central Statistics Office (2018a) *Productivity in Ireland, 2016*. Dublin: Central Statistics Office.

Central Statistics Office (2018b) *Population and Labour Force Projections 2017–2051*. Dublin: Central Statistics Office.

Central Statistics Office (2018c) *Innovation in Irish Enterprises*. Dublin: Central Statistics Office.

Chang, Ha-Joon (2014) *Economics: The User's Guide*. London: Penguin Books.

Collins, Micheál (2014) 'Total Direct and Indirect Tax Contributions of Households in Ireland: Estimates and Policy Simulations.' NERI Working Paper no. 18. Dublin: NERI.

Collins, Micheál (2016) 'Employees on the Minimum Wage in the Republic of Ireland.' NERI Working Paper no. 37. Dublin: NERI

Connors, Jenny, Ryan Duffy and Frank Newman (2016) 'Budgetary Impact of Changing Demographics 2017–2027.' Dublin: Irish Government Economic and Evaluation Service, Department of Public Expenditure and Reform.

Cumbers, Andrew (2017) 'Diversifying Public Ownership.' Online paper, https://thenextsystem.org/diversifying-public-ownership, accessed on 11 March 2019. The Next System Project.

Dalton, Pádraig (2014) 'The Story Behind Some of the Numbers.' Presentation to NERI Annual May Day Labour Market Conference, University College Cork.

Daly, Mary (2017) 'The First Dáil' in John Crowley, Dónal Ó Drisceoil and Mike Murphy (eds) *Atlas of the Irish Revolution*. Cork: Cork University Press.

Denny, Eleanor (2014) 'Energy Sector and Environmental Issues' in John O'Hagan and Carol Newman (eds) *The Economy of Ireland: National and Sectoral Policy Issues*. Dublin: Gill and Macmillan.

Department of Enterprise, Trade and Investment (2009) 'Management Matters in Northern Ireland and the Republic of Ireland.' In joint sponsorship with the Department for Employment and Learning, Invest NI, InterTrade Ireland and Forfás.

Department for the Economy (2017) *Economy 2030: a Consultation on an Industrial Strategy for Northern Ireland*. Belfast: Department for the Economy.

Department of Finance (2018) 'Patterns of Firm Level Productivity in Ireland. A Technical Background Paper for the Economic Development Review Committee.' Dublin: Department of Finance.

DGB Confederation of German Trade Unions (2012) 'A Marshall Plan for Europe Proposal by the DGB for an Economic Stimulus, Investment and Development Programme for Europe.'

Donovan, Dónal and Antóin E. Murphy (2013) *The Fall of the Celtic Tiger: Ireland and the Euro Debt Crisis*. Oxford: Open University Press.

Duggan, Vic (2013) 'Ireland's Investment Crisis: Diagnosis and Prescription.' NERI Working Paper no. 3. Dublin: NERI.

Erhard, Ludwig (1958) *Prosperity Through Competition*, London: Thames & Hudson.

European Environment Agency (2018) 'EEA Greenhouse Gas – data viewer.'

Erixon, Lennart (2008) *The Rehn-Meidner Model in Sweden: Its Rise, Challenges and Survival*. Stockholm: Department of Economics.

European Parliament (2017) 'Towards a Circular Economy – Waste Management in the EU.'

Folbre, Nancy (1994) *Who Pays for the Kids? Gender and the Structures of Constraint*. London: Routledge.

Frey, Carl B. and Michael A. Osborne (2017) 'Future of Employment: How Susceptible Are Jobs to Computerisation.' *Technological Forecasting and Social Change*. 114(C): 254–80.

Friedman, Milton (2009) *Capitalism and Freedom*. Chicago: Chicago University Press.

Gershuny, Jonathan and John Robinson (1988) 'Historical Changes in the Household Division of Labor.' *Demography*. November 1988, 25(4): 537–52.

Gold, Lorna (2018) *Climate Generation: Awakening to our Children's Future*. Dublin: Veritas.

Goldrick-Kelly, Paul and Tom Healy (2017) 'Ireland's Housing Emergency: Time for a Game Changer.' NERI Working Paper no. 41. Dublin: NERI.

Goldrick-Kelly, Paul and Tom McDonnell (2017) 'Taxation and Revenue Sufficiency in the Republic of Ireland.' NERI Working Paper no. 48. Dublin: NERI.

Goldrick-Kelly, Paul and Tom Healy (2018) 'Equality in Irish Healthcare: Time for a New Deal.' NERI Working Paper no. 54. Dublin: NERI.

Goldrick-Kelly, Paul and Paul Mac Flynn (2018) 'Productivity on the Island of Ireland: A Tale of Three Economies.' NERI Working Paper no. 57. Dublin: NERI.

Gylfason, Thorvaldur (2001) 'Natural Resources, Education, and Economic Development.' *European Economic Review*. 45(4–6): 847–59.

Haldane, Andrew (2016) 'The Costs of Short-termism' in Michael Jacobs and Mariana Mazzucato (eds) (2016) *Rethinking Capitalism:*

Economics and Policy for Sustainable and Inclusive Growth. London: Wiley Blackwell.

Hall, Peter and David Soskice (eds) (2001) *Varieties of Capitalism: The Institutional Foundations of Comparative Advantage.* Oxford: Oxford University Press.

Healy, Tom and Slowey, Maria (2006) 'Social Exclusion and Adult Engagement in Lifelong Learning: Some Comparative Implications for European States Based on Ireland's Celtic Tiger Experience.' *Compare: British Association for International and Comparative Education,* 36 (3): 359–78.

Healy, Seán, Sara Bourke, Ann Leahy, Eamon Murphy, Michelle Murphy and Brigid Reynolds (2016) *Choices for Equity and Sustainability: Securing Solidarity and the Common Good.* Dublin: Social Justice Ireland.

Hearne, Rory (2011) *Public Private Partnerships in Ireland: Failed Experiment or the Way Forward?* Manchester: Manchester University Press.

Hinarejos, Alicia (2008) 'The Right to Collective Action Versus EU Fundamental Freedoms.' *Human Rights Law Review.* 8(4): 714–29

Houses of the Oireachtas (2017a) *Sláintecare Report.* Dublin: Committee on the Future of Healthcare.

Houses of the Oireachtas (2017b) *Brexit and the Future of Ireland Uniting Ireland an Its People in Peace and Prosperity.* Dublin: Joint Committee on the Implementation of the Good Friday Agreement.

IMPACT (2017) *A Just Transition to a Low-Carbon Economy Implications for IMPACT and Its Members.* Drafted with support from IIEA. Dublin: Impact Trade Union.

Institute for Public Policy Research (2018) *Prosperity with Justice: A Plan for the New Economy.* The final Report of the IPPR Commission on Economic Justice.

Intergovernmental Panel on Climate Change (2018) *Summary for Policy Makers.*

InterTradeIreland (2015) *Mapping the Potential for All-Island Ecosystems.* Newry: InterTradeIreland.

Irish Congress of Trade Unions (2017a) *'Insecure and Uncertain': Precarious Work in the Republic of Ireland and Northern Ireland.* Dublin: Irish Congress of Trade Unions.

Irish Congress of Trade Unions (2017b) *Because We're Worth It: The Truth about CEO Pay in Ireland*. Dublin: Irish Congress of Trade Unions

Jacobson, David (2013) *The Nuts and Bolts of Innovation: New perspectives on Irish Industrial Policy*. TASC. Dublin: Glasnevin Publishing.

Jacobs, Michael and Mariana Mazzucato (eds) (2016) *Rethinking Capitalism: Economics and Policy for Sustainable and Inclusive Growth*. London: Wiley Blackwell.

Jenkins, Craig J., Kevin T. Leicht and Arthur Jaynes (2008) 'Creating High-Technology Growth: High-Tech Employment in US Metropolitan Areas, 1988–1998.' *Social Science Quarterly*. 89(2): 456–81.

Juncker, Jean-Claude (2015) *Completing Europe's Economic and Monetary Union* ('The Five Presidents' Report'). Brussels: European Commission.

Katzenstein, Peter (1985) *Small States in World Markets: Industrial Policy in Europe*. New York: Cornell University Press.

Kennedy, Kieran and Tom Healy (1985) *Small-Scale Manufacturing Industry in Ireland*. Paper no. 125. Dublin: Economic and Social Research Institute.

Kinsella, Stephen (2009) *Ireland in 2050: How We Will Be Living*. Dublin: Liberties Press.

Kirby, Peadar and Mary P. Murphy (2011) *Towards a Second Republic: Irish Politics after the Celtic Tiger*. London: Pluto Press.

Lakey, George (2017) *Viking Economics: How the Scandinavians Got it Right and How We Can, Too*. London: Melville House.

Lawless, Martina and Donal Lynch (2016) 'Scenarios and Distributional Implications of a Household Wealth Tax in Ireland.' ESRI Working Paper No 549. Dublin: NERI.

Lynch, Patrick (1994) '1894–1994: An Overview.' In Donal Nevin (ed) *Trade Union Century*. Dublin: Irish Congress of Trade Unions.

Mac Flynn, Paul (2016) 'Productivity and the Northern Ireland Economy.' NERI Working Paper no. 39. Dublin: NERI.

Mac Flynn, Paul and Lisa Wilson (2018) 'Housing Provision in Northern Ireland and its Implications for Living Standards and Poverty.' NERI Working Paper no. 52. Dublin: NERI.

Mac Gréil, Micheál, S.J. (2010) *Emancipation of the Travelling People*. Maynooth: NUI Maynooth.

Marx, Karl (1887) *Capital. A Critique of Political Economy. Volume 1*. First English-language edition.

Mason, Paul (2015) *Postcapitalism: A Guide to our Future*. London: Penguin.

McCabe, Conor (2013) 'Transforming Capitalism through Real Utopias: A Critical Engagement.' *Irish Journal of Sociology*. 21(2): 51–61.

McCabe, Conor (2017) *Irish Commonwealth: Trade Unions and Civil Society in the 21st Century*. Online publication. http://dublinopinion.com/2017/11/18/irish-commonwealth-trade-unions-and-civil-society-in-the-21st-century/, accessed 11 March 2019.

McDonnell, John (2018) *Economics for the Many*. London: Verso.

McDonnell, Thomas (2013) 'Wealth Tax: Options for its Implementation in the Republic of Ireland.' NERI Working Paper no. 13. Dublin: NERI.

McDonnell, Thomas (2014) 'Assessing Funding Models for Water Services Provision in Ireland.' NERI Working Paper no. 21. Dublin: NERI.

McDonnell, Thomas (2017) 'Innovative Competence: How does the Republic of Ireland Fare and does it Matter?', NERI Working Paper, no. 40. Dublin: NERI.

McDonnell, Thomas and Rory O'Farrell (2015) 'Internal Devaluation and Labour Market Trends during Ireland's Economic Crisis.' NERI Working Paper no. 28. Dublin: NERI.

Mettenheim, Kurt and Olivier Butzbach (2015) *Alternative Banking and Theory*. Accounting, Economics and Law 5(2): 105–71.

National Economic and Social Council (2005) *The Developmental Welfare State*, no. 113. Dublin: NESC.

Nedelkoska, Ljubica and Glenda Quintini (2018) 'Automation, Skills Use and Training.' OECD Social, Employment and Migration Working Papers, no. 202. Paris: OECD.

Nolan, Stephen, Eleonore Perrin Massebiaux and Tomas Gorman (2013) 'Saving Jobs, Promoting Democracy: Worker Co-operatives' in *Irish Journal of Sociology*. 21(2): 103–15.

Northern Ireland Public Service Alliance (2013) *Their System's Crisis: Our Fightback*. Belfast: NIPSA.

Northern Ireland Statistics and Research Agency (2018a) *2016-Based Population Projections for Northern Ireland*.

Northern Ireland Statistics and Research Agency (2018b) *Structure and Performance of the Northern Ireland Economy, 2014 and 2015*.

Nugent, Ciarán (2017) 'A Time-Series Analysis of Precarious Work in the Elementary Professions In Ireland.' NERI Working Paper no. 43. Dublin: NERI.

Nugent, Ciarán (2018) 'Wage Sufficiency in the Context of the Irish Housing Emergency: Rents and Access to Homeownership.' NERI Working Paper no. 51. Dublin: NERI.

O'Hanlon, Gerry (ed) (2017) *A Dialogue of Hope: Critical Thinking for Critical Times*. Dublin: Messenger Publications.

O'Hearn, Denis (2001) *The Atlantic Economy: Britain, the US and Ireland*. Manchester: Manchester University Press.

Ogle, Brendan (2016) *From Bended Knee to a New Republic: How the Fight for Water is Changing Ireland*. Dublin: Liffey Press.

Organisation for Economic Cooperation and Development (2001) *The Well-Being of Nations, the Role of Human and Social Capital*. Centre for Educational Research and Innovation, Paris: OECD.

Organisation for Economic Cooperation and Development (2013) *OECD Economics Surveys: Ireland 2013*.

Organisation for Economic Cooperation and Development (2015) *The Future of Productivity*. Paris: OECD.

O'Rafferty, Simon (2017) *Moving Towards the Circular Economy: Irish Case Studies*. Dublin: National Economic and Social Council.

Ó Riain, Seán (2004) *The Politics of High-Tech Growth: Developmental Network States in the Global Economy* (Structural Analysis in the Social Sciences 23). Cambridge UK: Cambridge University Press.

Ó Riain, Seán (2014) *The Rise and Fall of Ireland's Celtic Tiger: Liberalism, Boom and Bust*. Cambridge, UK: Cambridge University Press.

Osberg, Lars (2001) 'Comparisons of Trends in GDP and Economic Well-being – The Impact of Social Capital,' in John Helliwell (ed) *The Contribution of Human and Social Capital to Sustained Economic Growth and Well-being: International Symposium Report*. Ottawa and Paris: Human Resources Development Canada and Organisation for Economic Cooperation and Development.

Palma, José Gabriel (2009) 'The Revenge of the Market on the Rentiers: Why Neo-liberal Reports of the End of History Turned Out to Be Premature.' *Cambridge Journal of Economics* 2009 (33): 829–69.

Porter, Michael (1990) *Competitive Advantage of Nations: Creating and Sustaining Superior Performance*. New York: The Free Press.

Regling, Klaus and Max Watson (2010) *A Preliminary Report on The Sources of Ireland's Banking Crisis*. Dublin: Government Publications Office.

Russell, Helen, Bertrand Maître and Dorothy Watson (2016) 'Factors Associated with the Risk of Work-related Illnesses.' ESRI Research Briefing, October 2016. Dublin: NERI.

Sen, Amartya (1985) *Commodities and Capabilities*. New York: Elsevier.

SIPTU (2017) *There Are No Jobs on a Dead Planet: What a Just Transition Means for Workers*. Dublin: SIPTU.

Stiglitz, Joseph (2016) *The Euro: How a Common Currency Threatens the Future of Europe*. London: W.W. Norton.

Streeck, Wolfgang (2014) *Buying Time: The Delayed Crisis of Democratic Capitalism*. London: Verso Books.

Sweeney, Paul (2013a) 'State Support for the Irish Enterprise Sector' in David Jacobson (ed) *The Nuts and Bolts of Innovation: New Perspectives on Irish Industrial Policy*. Dublin: Glasnevin Publishing.

Sweeney, Paul (2013b) 'An Inquiry into the Declining Labour Share of National Income and the Consequences for Economies and Societies.' *Journal of the Statistical and Social Inquiry Society of Ireland*. 42.

Taft, Michael (2018) *Fat Cat Wednesday*, https://notesonthefront.type-pad.com/politicaleconomy/2019/01/its-fat-cat-wednesday.html, accessed 11 March 2019.

Turnbull, Daragh (2018) 'Housing Affordability for Ireland's Young People in the Context of the Cost of Living: A Long-Term Assessment.' NERI Working Paper no. 56. Dublin: NERI.

Wahl, Asbjørn (2011) *The Rise and Fall of the Welfare State*. London: Pluto Press.

White, Rossa (2010) *Years of High Income Largely Wasted*. Dublin: Davy Stockbrokers.

Wilkinson, Richard and Kate Pickett (2009) *The Spirit Level: Why Greater Equality Makes Societies Stronger*. New York: Bloomsbury Press.

Wilson, Lisa (2017) 'The Gendered Nature of Employment and Insecure Employment in Northern Ireland: A Story of Continuity and Change.' NERI Working Paper no. 50. Dublin: NERI.

Wright, Erik Olin (2013) 'Transforming Capitalism through Real Utopias.' *Irish Journal of Sociology*. 21(2): 6–40.

Endnotes

1   https://www.oireachtas.ie/en/debates/debate/dail/1919-01-21/15/, accessed 11 March 2019.

2   As well as other countries – not least the United States of America.

3   Otherwise known as the Good Friday Agreement.

4   Karl Marx wrote in *Kapital* (Marx, 1887, p. 485): 'Ireland is at present only an agricultural district of England, marked off by a wide channel from the country to which it yields corn, wool, cattle, industrial and military recruits.'

5   A lesson in future recessions is that a key challenge for public policy is to 'recycle' deficits by holding levels of domestic consumption and productive investment and reducing the public sector deficit over time by allowing the economy to grow again.

6   The Bank of England printed more money.

7   Knowledge box is a term applied to tax relief on income from qualifying patents, computer programmes and, for smaller companies, particular forms of intellectual property (IP).

8   'Base erosion and profit shifting (BEPS) refers to tax avoidance strategies that exploit gaps and mismatches in tax rules to artificially shift profits to low or no-tax locations.' See http://www.oecd.org/tax/beps/.

9   Analysis of Structural Business Statistics using Eurostat data indicates relative stability in total employment and total personnel costs over the period of the economic downturn. Refer to Eurostat Databank, code [fats_g1a_08].

10 Refer to the Eurostat online databank for productivity information and a more detailed analysis at refined sectoral level.

11 These observations on business start-ups and survival as well as patent applications are based on the latest available Eurostat data and

will be outlined and considered in more detail in forthcoming NERI research work on the role of domestic enterprises.

12   At the heart of Ireland's financial crisis were close ties between domestic banks and a small group of property developers in both residential and commercial property. Together, they misallocated capital in Ireland on a grand scale.

13   Bradley and Best (2012, p. 84) noted that the entirely sustainable expansion of the manufacturing sector that took place during the 1990s (the 'real' Celtic Tiger period) was replaced by a completely unsustainable expansion of non-internationally traded activities in the market service sector (the 'false' Celtic Tiger period).

14   Ó Riain (2014, p. 93) wrote: 'Buyers and sellers chased the market in an increasing volume of sales while credit grew rapidly – most of the long-term damage to the economy was done in a relatively short number of years between 2002 and 2008, even if the conditions for a bubble had been put in place before the 2000s.'

15   The abolition of the 'windfall tax' on profits from newly rezoned land in Budget 2015 signalled a return to policies that were instrumental in helping to bring about the crash.

16   The speech is no longer available online but was obtained on request by the author to the Department of Finance.

17   Refer to the statement arising from the British Academy Global Financial Crisis Forum in 2009.

18   Although there is a distinction between the 'crazy' phase of 2001–07 and the more sustainable boom of 1993–2000, much of the liberalisation measures that paved the way for the latter phase were already en route during the 1990s.

19   Legal developments in late 2018 confirm that the Irish government will reimburse junior bondholders many of whom took a hit initially.

20   Compensation of employees (wages and salaries, benefits in kind, employers' social insurance contribution).

21   For example, social welfare payments to the unemployed or retired.

22   Examples of deprivation include the lack of money to heat a home; to buy presents for family members; to afford a pair of shoes or a meal with meat or fish every second day; to afford a warm, waterproof coat or to afford to replace any worn-out furniture.

23   From unpublished data provided to the author by the Central Statistics Office.

24   The components add to 100 when the negative value attached to the
     bottom 20 per cent is included.

25   Presentation by Reamonn Lydon and Tara McIndoe-Calder at a NERI
     seminar in April 2015. https://www.nerinstitute.net/download/pdf/
     neri_22_april_2015_copy.pdf?issuusl=ignore

26   Estimates for individual consumption are not readily available for
     Northern Ireland but based on data published by the Northern Ireland
     Statistics and Research Agency, AIC is similar in Northern Ireland and
     the Republic of Ireland. Estimated GDP per capita was around 77 per
     cent of that for the UK as a whole in 2014 (Northern Ireland Statistics
     and Research Agency, 2018b). If a similar ratio is applied to Northern
     Ireland and the UK as a whole then AIC per capita is probably similar
     in the Republic of Ireland and Northern Ireland.

27   For a review of the literature on human well-being and the contri-
     bution of human and social capital, see Organisation for Economic
     Cooperation and Development (2001).

28   http://hdr.undp.org/en/content/human-development-index-hdi,
     accessed 11 March 2019.

29   Euro currency in notes and coins was issued from 2002.

30   Erhard stated in his 1958 book, *Prosperity Through Competition*, that
     'to increase prosperity by expansion than to try for a different dis-
     tribution of then national income by pointless ... It is considerably
     easier to allow everyone a larger slice out of a bigger cake than to
     gain anything by discussing the division of a smaller cake.' (Erhard,
     1958, pp. 3–4).

31   For a more detailed explanation of these cases see Hinarejos (2008).

32   A fiscal transfer union among countries is similar to arrangements in,
     for example, the US or the UK where one state or country subvents
     another.

33   Such as the break-up of Yugoslavia and the continuing conflict in the
     Ukraine.

34   And to these three may be added a multitude of 'identity' politics
     and belonging from single-issue stances to more traditional class- or
     tribal-based belongings.

35   These terms were coined in 2002 by Donald Rumsfeld, former US
     Secretary of State for Defence.

36   In the labour market, provision should be made to protect all workers'
     rights and conditions and levels of pay. Immigration should not be
     used to undermine gains made in these areas.

37 Only one scenario in relation to mortality was used by the CSO.

38 Includes public pensions, health and education.

39 On the assumption of a fall in labour force participation and a modest level of net outward migration.

40 Under a slow growth scenario, the number of 85-year-olds and over is projected to rise from 67,300 persons in 2016 (or 1.4 per cent of total population) to 298,200 persons (or 5.3 per cent of the total) in 2051.

41 http://ec.europa.eu/clima/change/causes/index_en.htm, accessed 11 March 2019.

42 Eurostat databank assessed in October 2018. Data refers to all man-made emissions of the so-called 'Kyoto basket' of greenhouse gases.

43 I am grateful to Professor John Barry of Queen's University Belfast who pointed out that the economist Simon Kuznets, one of the early pioneers in the conceptualisation of GDP or national income, argued for the exclusion of certain socially undesirable activities – economic in nature but not contributing to human well-being. At the same time, Kuznets made the case for including economic activities crucial to overall well-being and 'productivity' such as domestic work outside the paid labour market. The decision about what to include in the concept and measure of GDP is a normative and not a purely statistical or methodological one.

44 Except in cases of slavery.

45 The Central Statistics Office publishes four alternative measures of under-employment. The most broadly defined measure is referred to as PLS4. This comprises the unemployed in addition to persons who want a job but are not available at a given time and who may not be seeking for reasons other than being in education.

46 There will always be some degree of what economists call 'frictional' unemployment or under-employment, whereby individuals are without work yet searching for work in between jobs over a short period of time. A rate of full employment is difficult to define or measure. In the decades following World War II most advanced economies experienced rates of unemployment in the region of 2 per cent or more. In more recent decades a level of 5 per cent is more typical at least during periods out of recession or stagnation.

47 Research by the Vincentian Partnership adopts a 'consensual budgets standards approach' whereby representative focus groups estimated budgets on the basis of a households minimum needs rather than wants. These budgets, spanning over 2,000 goods, were developed

for sixteen areas of expenditure. The analysis distinguishes between expenditure for urban and rural households.

48   Refer to http://livingwage.ie/

49   Confusion about terminology is not helped by the equation of the UK national statutory minimum wage to the national living wage. In April 2018 the national statutory minimum wage for 21-year-olds and upwards was £7.83, well below the estimated living wage of £8.75 per hour outside of London, including Northern Ireland.

50   Matthew 26:11.

51   Recent experimental research on the implementation of UBI in Finland has indicated no evidence of employment gains. However, some increase in personal well-being was found. It is impossible to generalise from this study in making a case for UBI across countries and settings.

52   Examples might include greater investment in cultural centres, support for cultural education and local cultural events.

53   The slow and incomplete implementation of the Vacant Site Levy is a matter of concern.

54   Based on numbers of children, assumed staff ratios, average salary levels and overhead costs.

55   The Northern European Comparator Group (NECG) is a selection of ten Northern or Central European countries that are members of the EU and have similar levels of economic prosperity. They are: Austria, Belgium, Denmark, Finland, Germany, France, the Republic of Ireland, the Netherlands, Sweden and the United Kingdom.

56   I am again grateful to Professor Barry for the following observation on an earlier draft of this work: 'Why do we not begin shaping a new economic vision by reversing the orthodox solution to the "needs/wants vs finite resources" issue by reducing wants and satisfying needs?'

57   For a discussion of the structure of taxation and spending see 'Things you always wanted to know about Northern Ireland public finances'.

58   'Public services make a shabby contrast with national wealth', *The Irish Times*, 22 March 2008.

59   Formally, GNI*, or modified GNI, corresponds to the value of gross national income less the income of companies re-domiciled to the Republic of Ireland in recent years and the value of depreciation of intellectual products as well as the value of activities by companies located in the Republic of Ireland and engaged in the leasing of aircraft.

60   http://press.conservatives.com/post/98719492085/george-osborne-speech-to-conservative-party

61   http://pdf.cso.ie/www/pdf/20171018103519_Business_Demography_2015_full.pdf, accessed 11 March 2019.

62   That is, where enterprises import much of their inputs and raw materials and export much of what they produce.

63   For an overview of the Danish model see Cumbers (2017).

64   Icelandic economist Thorvaldur Gylfason (2001, p. 64) writes that such nations may 'develop a false sense of security and become negligent about the accumulation of human capital'.

65   Porter's views (1990, p. 671) are relevant here: 'Except when it is largely passive, widespread foreign investment usually indicates that the process of competitive upgrading in an economy is not entirely healthy because domestic firms in many industries lack the capabilities to defend their market positions against foreign firms … Inbound foreign investment is never the solution to a nation's competitive problems.'

66   Acceptance speech by President Higgins as reported in *The Irish Times*.

67   https://www.ictu.ie/download/pdf/congress_constitution_standing_orders_oct_2017.pdf, accessed 11 March 2019.

68   In 1998 an overwhelming majority of people in the Republic of Ireland voted to incorporate the following new wording of Article 3 of the Irish Constitution: 'It is the firm will of the Irish Nation, in harmony and friendship, to unite all the people who share the territory of the island of Ireland, in all the diversity of their identities and traditions, recognising that a united Ireland shall be brought about only by peaceful means with the consent of a majority of the people, democratically expressed, in both jurisdictions in the island.'

69   COMECON, which lasted from 1949 to 1991 stood for Council for Mutual Economic Assistance and was a USSR-led association of communist states in Eastern Europe as well as Mongolia and Vietnam.

70   The expression 'socialism or barbarism' was used by the German communist, Rosa Luxemburg, whose 1915 'Junius' pamphlet was ironically entitled *The Crisis of German Social Democracy*.

Index

About the Author

Tom Healy is director of the Nevin Economic Research Institute (NERI). He has previously worked in the Economic and Social Research Institute (ESRI), the Northern Ireland Economic Research Centre, the Organisation for Economic Cooperation and Development, the National Economic and Social Forum and the Department of Education and Skills. He holds a PhD (economics and sociology) from University College Dublin. His research interests include the impact of education and social capital on well-being, housing, healthcare and a social vision and economic strategy for the island of Ireland. He writes a regular blog, *Monday Blog*, at nerinstitute.net/blog/author/tomhealy/.